215993

1st EDITION

Perspectives on Diseases and Disorders

Sexually Transmitted Diseases

Clay Farris Naff
Book Editor

Detroit • New York • San Francisco • New Haven, Conn • Waterville, Maine • London

Grand Island Public Library

Christine Nasso, *Publisher*
Elizabeth Des Chenes, *Managing Editor*

© 2009 Greenhaven Press, a part of Gale, Cengage Learning

Gale and Greenhaven Press are registered trademarks used herein under license.

For more information, contact:
Greenhaven Press
27500 Drake Rd.
Farmington Hills, MI 48331-3535
Or you can visit our Internet site at gale.cengage.com

ALL RIGHTS RESERVED.
No part of this work covered by the copyright herein may be reproduced, transmitted, stored, or used in any form or by any means graphic, electronic, or mechanical, including but not limited to photocopying, recording, scanning, digitizing, taping, Web distribution, information networks, or information storage and retrieval systems, except as permitted under Section 107 or 108 of the 1976 United States Copyright Act, without the prior written permission of the publisher.

For product information and technology assistance, contact us at

Gale Customer Support, 1-800-877-4253
For permission to use material from this text or product, submit all requests online at www.cengage.com/permissions

Further permissions questions can be emailed to permissionrequest@cengage.com

Articles in Greenhaven Press anthologies are often edited for length to meet page requirements. In addition, original titles of these works are changed to clearly present the main thesis and to explicitly indicate the author's opinion. Every effort is made to ensure that Greenhaven Press accurately reflects the original intent of the authors. Every effort has been made to trace the owners of copyrighted material.

Cover image copyright Sebastian Kaulitzki. Used under license of Shutterstock.com.

LIBRARY OF CONGRESS CATALOGING-IN-PUBLICATION DATA

Sexually transmitted diseases / Clay Farris Naff, book editor.
    p. cm. — (Perspectives on diseases and disorders)
  Includes bibliographical references and index.
  ISBN 978-0-7377-4248-0 (hardcover)
 1. Sexually transmitted diseases. I. Naff, Clay Farris.
  RC200.25.S482 2009
  616.95'1—dc22

                                                                  2008031525

Printed in the United States of America
1 2 3 4 5 6 7 12 11 10 09 08

CONTENTS

INTRODUCTION

Sexually transmitted diseases, or STDs, are among the most common and least talked about afflictions. By some estimates, half of all people will contract an STD at some point in their lives, yet almost no one speaks of having one. In this way, STDs are unique among infectious diseases.

Nobody hides the fact that they have caught a cold. The chicken pox causes misery, but it does not give rise to elaborate lies. Why should chlamydia, herpes, or syphilis be so different? The reasons are fairly straightforward, but the consequences are complex.

Sexuality is at the core of our beings, and never more so than in the years when STDs are most likely to strike: adolescence and young adulthood. During the transition from childhood to the teen years, biological development drives young people into competition for social status. This competition can take many forms—athletics, academics, clothing, music, dance styles, cliques, and bullying, to name a few. Underlying all of these is the competition to be regarded as sexy, a status that is summed up in the quintessential teen word, "cool."

Most infectious diseases are irrelevant to this competition, but a sexually transmitted disease can be a considerable handicap. In fact, with few exceptions, people who learn that they have an STD react with feelings of shame, confusion, and fear about how others will regard them.

"The first year I was ashamed, got flare ups all the time, and didn't have anybody that I trusted to talk to about what was happening in my life," writes an Omaha resident who contracted herpes at the age of 25.[1] She eventually adopted the screen name "Yoshi2me" and started an online support group for others with the disease.

Denial Delays Treatment

The tendency to be silent about STDs has many unfortunate consequences. Many people are reluctant to admit to themselves that they may be infected. Gayla Baer McCord, a work-at-home mom from Indiana, suffered for a year and half with what she thought were recurrent bladder infections. It took unbearable pain to force her to accept that she had something worse. "I awoke one summer June morning and prepared for a fun-filled road adventure to a race being held in Ohio . . . While at the race, I felt pains like none I had never experienced before. At the risk of being too blunt, I felt as if I was urinating razor blades."[2] McCord was ultimately diagnosed with genital herpes.

The Healthy Youth Act, a state law in Washington, does not require schools to teach sex education, but it sets a standard for schools that do. (AP Images)

Shame, denial, and ignorance cause a significant number of STDs to go undiagnosed. Obviously, no one knows just how many, but various studies involving anonymous surveys and urine samples from teens who have not received a diagnosis establish the reality of overlooked STDs. A 2001 study at the Magee-Womens Research Institute in Pittsburgh, Pennsylvania, found nearly one in five previously undiagnosed teen girls had an STD. A 2008 study by the U.S. Centers for Disease Control and Prevention (CDC) suggests that the news may be getting worse: It found that one in four teenage girls has an STD.

The failure to have an STD diagnosed and treated can be tragic. In women, especially, curable STDs such as chlamydia can cause sterility if left to fester. "Untreated infection can spread into the uterus or fallopian tubes and cause pelvic inflammatory disease (PID)," the CDC warns. "This happens in up to 40 percent of women with untreated chlamydia. PID can cause permanent damage to the fallopian tubes, uterus, and surrounding tissues. The damage can lead to chronic pelvic pain, infertility, and potentially fatal ectopic pregnancy (pregnancy outside the uterus)."[3]

The tendency to engage in denial often rises with the severity of the disease. The most frightening and, for many, stigmatizing of all STDs is human immunodeficiency virus, or HIV, the virus that causes AIDS. Despite more than twenty years of intensive research, it remains incurable, and while treatments have greatly improved the odds of surviving for a long time, to be infected with HIV is a life-changing experience that ultimately proves fatal. Small wonder then that many people go into denial when they learn (or suspect) that they have contracted HIV.

Babies Become Victims

The worst consequence of denial is that it not only delays the onset of treatment but also allows the disease to spread to unwitting partners—or others. Needle-sharing, accidental transfers of infected blood from one person to another,

The HPV vaccine is a groundbreaking vaccine that prevents cervical cancer in girls. This eighteen-year-old receives her third and final application of the vaccine. (**AP Images**)

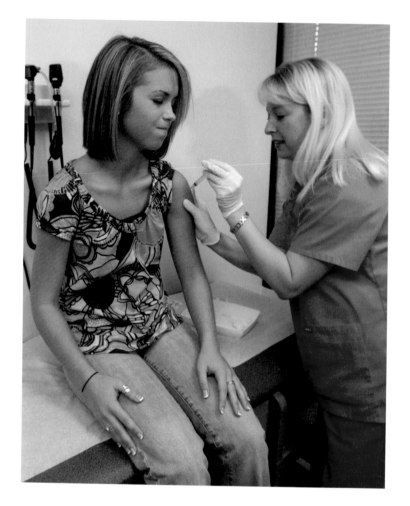

or even organ transplants can be the means of transmission, but by far the most common nonsexual way an STD slips from an infected person to another is through pregnancy.

An estimated 10 percent of pregnant women in America are infected with chlamydia, the most common of STDs. Herpes, while not as common generally, infects an estimated 22 percent of pregnant women. Medical screening can identify these and other STDs, and early intervention can usually prevent transmission of the infection to the fetus. Sadly, however, researchers say that the majority of women—especially young women most likely to be infected—do not undergo screening.

As a result, millions of babies are born at risk of life-threatening complications from STDs. Chlamydia and herpes can both cause blindness in a newborn. HIV frequently leads to early death. Massive public awareness campaigns have greatly reduced the number of HIV-positive babies born each year, from a high of two thousand annually in the early 1990s to roughly two hundred a year at present, but the numbers are still a dismal testament to the power of denial.

For some, denial shifts from the infection to its effects. A small but vocal minority claim that HIV is a harmless virus that has nothing to do with AIDS. Relying on the claims of maverick biochemist Peter Duesberg, they argue that AIDS is not an infectious disease but a lifestyle disorder.

Early on in the epidemic, this represented a genuine alternative hypothesis. In the decades since, an overwhelming body of scientific evidence has confirmed the HIV-AIDS link, but that has not stopped the deniers. Their delusion has tragic consequences. To pick one example of many, in 2005 Eliza Jane Scovill, the three-year-old daughter of HIV-positive author Christine Maggiore, died of complications from AIDS.

The book that made her mother famous was a tract rejecting medical treatment for HIV. Maggiore refused treatment while pregnant and so passed the virus on to her daughter. Even after Eliza Jane's death, she refused to accept the role of HIV.

"I have been brought to my emotional knees, but not in regard to the science of this topic," Maggiore told the *Los Angeles Times*. "I am a devastated, broken, grieving mother, but I am not second-guessing or questioning my understanding of the issue."[4]

Thrill Seekers

Just because sex can be risky does not mean that teenagers will avoid it. On the contrary, risk is never more attractive than during the teen years. The result is that most American teenagers engage in sex before they graduate from high school, and many gamble with their health in doing so. Attempts to deter teen sex through "abstinence only" programs have had no positive effect, according to research. As one study notes, "Adolescents are at increased risk of STD because they are more likely to engage in such risk-taking behaviors as unprotected sex, multiple sexual partners and sexual relationships of short duration."[5]

Among some gay men, there is a morbid fascination with HIV-positive status, with the result that all too many engage in unprotected sex. "I guess I don't ask every time," a man identified only as "Bob" admits. "I've been ultra lucky. I don't know why I do it, except that it feels great."[6]

In sum, what sets STDs apart from other infectious diseases is the silence, ignorance, recklessness, lies, and self-deception associated with them. The tragedy is that disease management has greatly improved in recent years. Experts agree that if people were able to be honest and forthright about the subject, the suffering caused by STDs would be

Volunteers from Planned Parenthood and other community organizations pass out free condoms to spring breakers at J.P. Luby Surf Park Beach in Corpus Christi, Texas. (AP Images)

greatly diminished. Although progress has been made in public awareness and stigma reduction, an era of socially responsible attitudes toward STDs remains a far-off hope. In the meantime, sexually transmitted infections continue to spread in silence.

Notes

1. Angela, "Herpes Biography," Sex Buzz. http://yoshi2me .com/herpes-biography.html.
2. Gayla Baer McCord, "My Story," November 15, 2003. www.herpesonline.org/mystory.html.
3. Centers for Disease Control and Prevention, "Chlamydia-CDC Fact Sheet," December 20, 2007. www .cdc.gov/std/Chlamydia/STDFact-Chlamydia.htm# complications.
4. Quoted in Charles Ornstein and Daniel Costello, "HIV Denialist's Daughter Dies of HIV," *Los Angeles Times*, September 24, 2005. www.natap.org/2005/newsUp dates/092705_02.htm.
5. Dawn M. Upchurch et al., "Social and Behavioral Determinants of Self-Reported STD Among Adolescents," *Perspectives on Sexual and Reproductive Health,* November 1, 2004.
6. Quoted in Mubarak Dahir, "Confessions of Barebacking, *Bay Windows,* December 11, 2003. ww1.aegis.org/ news/bayw/2003/BY031202.html.

CHAPTER 1

Understanding Sexually Transmitted Diseases

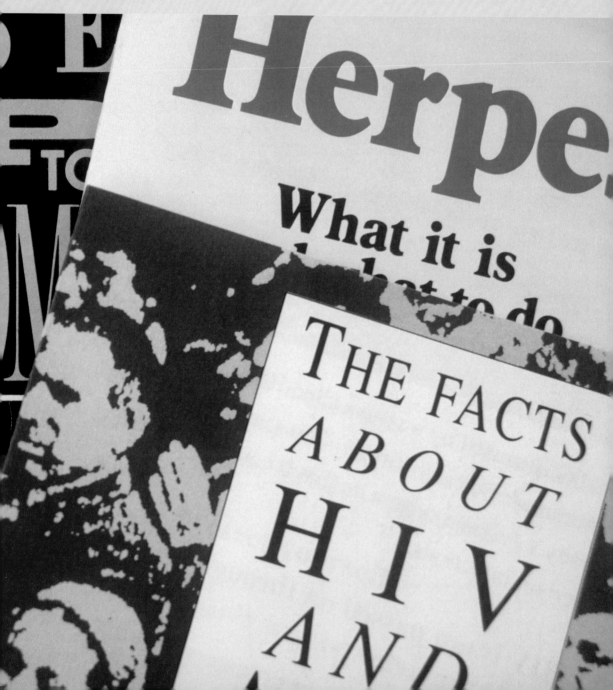

An Overview of Sexually Transmitted Diseases

Maureen Haggerty

Sexually transmitted diseases, or STDs, are among the most common and least discussed of infectious illnesses. In the following article selection writer Maureen Haggerty explains that the term STD covers at least twenty different diseases. Some make themselves obvious; others frequently go undetected. All are potentially harmful. Some, as she explains, can cause brain damage, heart disease, or even death. Many STDs are treatable, though not necessarily curable. Those that are caused by bacteria can, for the most part, be overcome by antibiotics. Viral diseases, however, may last a lifetime, though the symptoms are often controlled. Maureen Haggerty is a writer in Bucks County in Eastern Pennsylvania. She frequently writes on medical topics.

Sexually transmitted disease (STD) is a term used to describe more than 20 different infections that are transmitted through exchange of semen, blood, and other body fluids; or by direct contact with the affected

SOURCE: Maureen Haggerty, *Gale Encyclopedia of Medicine*, 3rd Edition. Belmont, CA: Gale, 2006. Copyright 2006 Gale, a part of Cengage Learning. Reproduced by permission of Gale, a part of Cengage Learning.

Photo on facing page. According to the Centers for Disease Control and Prevention, more than 15 million cases of sexually transmitted diseases are reported each year. (Christine Osborne Pictures/Alamy)

body areas of people with STDs. Sexually transmitted diseases are also called venereal diseases.

The Centers for Disease Control and Prevention (CDC) has reported that 85% of the most prevalent infectious diseases in the United States are sexually transmitted. The rate of STDs in this country is 50 to 100 times higher than that of any other industrialized nation. One in four sexually active Americans will be affected by an STD at some time in his or her life.

About 12 million new STD infections occur in the United States each year. One in four occurs in someone between the ages of 16 and 19. Almost 65% of all STD infections affect people under the age of 25.

Types of STDs

STDs can have very painful long-term consequences as well as immediate health problems. They can cause:

- birth defects
- blindness
- bone deformities
- brain damage
- cancer
- heart disease
- infertility and other abnormalities of the reproductive system
- mental retardation
- death

Some of the most common and potentially serious STDs in the United States include:

Chlamydia. This STD is caused by the bacterium *Chlamydia trachomatis*, a microscopic organism that lives as a parasite inside human cells. Although over 526,000 cases of chlamydia were reported in the United States in 1997, the CDC estimates that nearly three million cases occur annually because 75% of women and 50% of men show no symptoms of the disease after infection. Approximately 40% of women will develop pelvic inflammatory disease (PID) as a result of chlamydia infection, a leading cause of infertility.

Human papillomavirus (HPV). HPV causes genital warts and is the single most important risk factor for cervical cancer in women. Over 100 types of HPV exist, but only about 30 of them can cause genital warts and are spread

Drugs Used to Treat STDs

Brand Name (Generic Name)	Possible Common Side Effects Include:
Achromycin V (tetracyline hydrochloride)	Blurred vision, headache, dizziness, rash, hives, appetite loss, nausea and vomiting
Amoxil (amoxicillin)	Behavioral changes, diarrhea, hives, nausea and vomiting
Ceftin (cefuroxime axetil)	Nausea and vomiting, diarrhea, irritated skin
Doryx (doxycycline hyclate)	Itching (genital and/or rectal), nausea and vomiting, appetite loss, diarrhea, swelling
E.E.S., E-Mycin, ERYC, Ery-Tab, Erythrocin, Ilosone (erythromycin)	Diarrhea, nausea and vomiting, appetite loss, abdominal pain
Flagyl (metronidazole)	Numbness, tingling sensation in extremities, seizures
Floxin (ofloxacin)	Genital itching, nausea and vomiting; headache, diarrhea, dizziness
Minocin (minocycline hydrochloride)	Blurred vision, anemia, hives, rash, throat irritation
Noroxin (norfloxacin)	Headache, nausea, dizziness
Omnipen (ampicillin)	Itching, rash, hives, peeling skin, nausea and vomiting
Penetrex (enoxacin)	Nausea and vomiting
Zithromax (azithromycin)	Nausea and vomiting, diarrhea, abdominal pain
Zovirax (acyclovir)	Fluid retention, headache, rash, tingling sensation

Taken from: *Gale Encyclopedia of Medicine*, vol. 4, 2006.

through sexual contact. In some instances, warts are passed from mother to child during childbirth, leading to a potentially life-threatening condition for newborns in which warts develop in the throat (laryngeal papillomatosis).

Genital herpes. Herpes is an incurable viral infection thought to be one of the most common STDs in this country. It is caused by one of two types of herpes simplex viruses: HSV-1 (commonly causing oral herpes) or HSV-2 (usually causing genital herpes). The CDC estimates that 45 million Americans (one out of every five individuals 12 years of age or older) are infected with HSV-2; this number has increased 30% since the 1970s. HSV-2 infection is more common in women (one out of every four women) than men (one out of every five men) and in African Americans (45.9%) than Caucasians (17.6%).

Gonorrhea. The bacterium *Neisseria gonorrhoeae* is the causative agent of gonorrhea and can be spread by vaginal, oral, or anal contact. The CDC reports that approximately 650,000 individuals are infected with gonorrhea each year in the United States, with 132.2 infections per 100,000 individuals occurring in 1999. Approximately 75% of American gonorrhea infections occur in persons aged 15 to 29 years old. In 1999, 75% of reported gonorrhea cases occurred among African Americans.

Syphilis. Syphilis is a potentially life-threatening infection that increases the likelihood of acquiring or transmitting HIV. In 1998, the CDC reported approximately 38,000 cases of syphilis in the United States; this included 800 cases of congenital syphilis. Congenital syphilis causes irreversible health problems or death in as many as 40% of all live babies born to women with untreated syphilis.

Human immunodeficiency virus (HIV) infection. In 2000, the CDC reported that 120,223 people in the United States are HIV-positive and 426,350 are living with AIDS. In addition, approximately 1,000–2,000 children are born each year with HIV infection. It is also estimated that 33 million adults and 1.3 million children worldwide were living with HIV/AIDS as of 1999 with 5.4 million being newly infected that year. There is no cure for this STD. . . .

Some Groups Are Affected More than Others

STDs affect certain population groups more severely than others. Women, young people, and members of minority groups are particularly affected. Women in any age bracket are more likely than men to develop medical complications related to STDs. With respect to racial and ethnic categories, the incidence of syphilis is 60 times higher among African Americans than among Caucasians, and four times higher in Hispanics than in Anglos. According to the CDC, in 1999 African Americans accounted for 77% of the total number of gonorrhea cases and nearly 46% of all genital herpes cases.

Symptoms Vary

The symptoms of STDs vary somewhat according to the disease agent (virus or bacterium), the sex of the patient, and the body systems affected. The symptoms of some STDs are easy to identify; others produce infections that may either go unnoticed for some time or are easy to confuse with other diseases. Syphilis in particular can be confused with disorders ranging from infectious mononucleosis to allergic reactions to prescription medications. In addition, the incubation period of STDs varies. Some produce symptoms close enough to the time of sexual contact—often less than 48 hours later—for the patient to recognize the connection between the behavior and the symptoms. Others have a longer incubation period, so that the patient may not recognize the early symptoms as those of a sexually transmitted infection.

Some symptoms of STDs affect the genitals and reproductive organs:

- A woman who has an STD may bleed when she is not menstruating or have abnormal vaginal discharge. Vaginal burning, itching, and odor are common, and she may experience pain in her pelvic area while having sex.

- A discharge from the tip of the penis may be a sign that a man has an STD. Males may also have painful or burning sensations when they urinate.

- There may be swelling of the lymph nodes near the groin area.

- Both men and women may develop skin rashes, sores, bumps, or blisters near the mouth or genitals. Homosexual men frequently develop these symptoms in the area around the anus.

Other symptoms of STDs are systemic, which means that they affect the body as a whole. These symptoms may include:

- fever, chills, and similar flu-like symptoms
- skin rashes over large parts of the body
- arthritis-like pains or aching in the joints
- throat swelling and redness that lasts for three weeks or longer

Diagnosis of STDs

A sexually active person who has symptoms of an STD or who has had an STD or symptoms of infection should be examined without delay by one of the following health care professionals:

- a specialist in women's health (gynecologist)
- a specialist in disorders of the urinary tract and the male sexual organs (urologist)
- a family physician
- a nurse practitioner
- a specialist in skin disorders (dermatologist)

The diagnostic process begins with a thorough physical examination and a detailed medical history that documents the patient's sexual history and assesses the risk of infection.

The doctor or other health care professional will:

• Describe the testing process. This includes all blood tests and other tests that may be relevant to the specific infection.

• Explain the meaning of the test results.

• Provide the patient with information regarding high-risk behaviors and any necessary treatments or procedures.

The doctor may suggest that a patient diagnosed with one STD be tested for others, as it's possible to have more than one STD at a time. One infection may hide the symptoms of another or create a climate that fosters its growth. At present, it is particularly important that persons who are HIV-positive be tested for syphilis as well.

The law in most parts of the United States requires public health officials to trace and contact the partners of persons with STDs. Minors, however, can get treatment without their parents' permission. Public health departments in most states can provide information about STD clinic locations; Planned Parenthood facilities provide testing and counseling. These agencies can also help with or assume the responsibility of notifying sexual partners who must be tested and may require treatment.

Treatment and Prognosis

Although self-care can relieve some of the pain of genital herpes or genital warts that has recurred after being diagnosed and treated by a physician, other STD symptoms require immediate medical attention.

Antibiotics are prescribed to treat gonorrhea, chlamydia, syphilis, and other STDs caused by bacteria. Although

> **FAST FACT**
>
> The United States has the highest rates of STDs in the industrialized world. Approximately 15.3 million new cases of STDs are reported in the United States each year.

STDs affect certain population groups more than others. The incidence of syphilis is sixty times higher among African Americans than among Caucasians and four times higher in Hispanics than Anglos. (Frances Roberts/Alamy)

prompt diagnosis and early treatment almost always cures these STDs, new infections can develop if exposure continues or is renewed. Viral infections can be treated symptomatically with antiviral medications.

The prognosis for recovery from STDs varies among the different diseases. The prognosis for recovery from gonorrhea, syphilis, and other STDs caused by bacteria is generally good, provided that the disease is diagnosed early and treated promptly. Untreated syphilis in particular can lead to long-term complications and disability. Viral STDs (genital herpes, genital warts, HIV) cannot be cured but must be treated on a long-term basis to relieve symptoms and prevent life-threatening complications.

Prevention

Vaccines for the prevention of hepatitis A and hepatitis B are currently recommended for gay and bisexual men, users of illegal drugs, health care workers, and others at risk of contracting these diseases. Vaccines to prevent other STDs are being tested and may be available within several years.

The risk of becoming infected with an STD can be reduced or eliminated by changing certain personal behaviors. Abstaining from sexual relations or maintaining a mutually monogamous relationship with a partner are legitimate options. It is also wise to avoid sexual contact with partners who are known to be infected with an STD, whose health status is unknown, who abuse drugs, or who are involved in prostitution.

Men or women who have sex with a partner of known (or unsure) infection should make sure a new condom is used every time they have genital, oral, or anal contact. Used correctly and consistently, male condoms provide good protection against HIV and other STDs such as gonorrhea, chlamydia, and syphilis. Female condoms (lubricated sheaths inserted into the vagina) have also been shown to be effective in preventing HIV and other STDs. Condoms provide a measure of protection against genital herpes, genital warts, and hepatitis B.

Spermicides and diaphragms can decrease the risk of transmission of some STDs. They do not protect women from contracting HIV. Birth-control pills, patches, or injections do not prevent STDs. Neither do surgical sterilization or hysterectomy.

Urinating and washing the genital area with soap and water immediately after having sex may eliminate some germs before they cause infection. Douching, however, can spread infection deeper into the womb. It may also increase a woman's risk of developing pelvic inflammatory disease (PID).

Trends in the Leading Sexually Transmitted Diseases

Centers for Disease Control and Prevention

The federal government's main agency for monitoring the spread of sexually transmitted diseases (STDs) is the Centers for Disease Control and Prevention, or CDC. The following excerpt from the CDC's annual report on STDs begins by noting two ominous facts: First, the spread of STDs is concentrated among young people. Indeed, nearly half the infections occur in patients between the ages of fifteen and twenty-four. Second, the data collected by the CDC is far from complete. Many more cases go undetected, and many people notice that something is wrong but fail to have their malady diagnosed. Of those STDs reported, three stand out in terms of the number of cases reported. Chlamydia, a bacterial disease that can cause sterility in women, leads the pack with more than a million cases reported per year. It is followed by gonorrhea and syphilis, which are also bacterial diseases with serious consequences. The Atlanta-based CDC is part of the U.S. Department of Health and Human Services. The CDC is the primary federal agency responsible for monitoring the spread of communicable disease and coordinating prevention and response to outbreaks.

SOURCE: Centers for Disease Control and Prevention, "STD Surveillance 2006," in cdc.gov, November 13, 2007.

S exually transmitted diseases [STDs] remain a major public health challenge in the United States. While substantial progress has been made in preventing, diagnosing, and treating certain STDs in recent years, CDC [Centers for Disease Control and Prevention] estimates that approximately 19 million new infections occur each year, almost half of them among young people ages 15 to 24. In addition to the physical and psychological consequences of STDs, these diseases also exact a tremendous economic toll. Direct medical costs associated with STDs in the United States are estimated at up to $14.7 billion annually in 2006 dollars.

This document summarizes 2006 national data on trends in three notifiable STDs—chlamydia, gonorrhea, and syphilis—that are published in CDC's report, *Sexually Transmitted Disease Surveillance 2006*. These data, which are useful for examining overall trends and trends among populations at risk, represent only a small proportion of the true national burden of STDs. Many cases of notifiable STDs go undiagnosed, and some highly prevalent viral infections, such as human papillomavirus and genital herpes, are not reported at all.

Chlamydia Is the Most Commonly Reported Infectious Disease

Chlamydia remains the most commonly reported infectious disease in the United States. In 2006, 1,030,911 chlamydia diagnoses were reported, up from 976,445 in 2005. Even so, most chlamydia cases go undiagnosed. It is estimated that there are approximately 2.8 million new cases of chlamydia in the United States each year.

The national rate of reported chlamydia in 2006 was 347.8 cases per 100,000 population, an increase of 5.6 percent from 2005 [329.4]. The increases in reported cases and rates likely reflect the continued expansion of screening efforts and increased use of more sensitive diagnostic tests; however, the continued increases may also reflect an actual increase in infections.

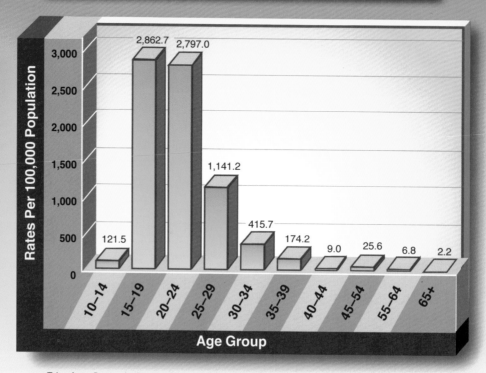

Chlamydia Rates Among Females, 2006

Rates Per 100,000 Population

- 10-14: 121.5
- 15-19: 2,862.7
- 20-24: 2,797.0
- 25-29: 1,141.2
- 30-34: 415.7
- 35-39: 174.2
- 40-44: 9.0
- 45-54: 25.6
- 55-64: 6.8
- 65+: 2.2

Age Group

Taken from: Centers for Disease Control and Prevention, "STD Surveillance 2006," November 13, 2007.

Young Women Bear the Brunt

Women, especially young women, are hit hardest by chlamydia. Studies have found that chlamydia is more common among adolescent females than adolescent males, and the long-term consequences of untreated disease are much more severe for females. The chlamydia case rate for females in 2006 was three times higher than for males [515.8 vs. 173.0]. Much of this difference reflects the fact that females are far more likely to be screened than males. Young females aged 15 to 19 had the highest chlamydia rate [2,862.7], followed by females aged 20 to 24 [2,797.0].

Chlamydia is common among all races and ethnic groups; however, African-American women are disproportionately affected. In 2006, the rate of reported chlamydia per 100,000 black females [1,760.9] was more than seven times that of white females [237.0] and more than twice that of Hispanic females [761.3]. The rate among American Indian/Alaska Native females was the second highest, at 1,262.3, and the rate among Asian/Pacific Islander females was the lowest, at 201.2.

Because case reports do not provide a complete account of the burden of disease, researchers also evaluate chlamydia prevalence in subgroups of the population to better estimate the true extent of the disease. For example, data from chlamydia screening in family planning clinics across the United States indicate that approximately 7 percent of 15- to 24-year-old females in these settings are infected.

The Importance of Screening

Because chlamydia is most common among young women, CDC recommends annual chlamydia screening for all sexually active women under age 26, as well as older women with risk factors such as new or multiple sex partners. Data from one study in a managed care setting suggest that chlamydia screening and treatment can reduce the incidence of pelvic inflammatory disease [PID] by over 50 percent. Unfortunately, many sexually active young women are not being tested for chlamydia, in part reflecting a lack of awareness among some providers and limited resources for screening. Research has shown that simple changes in clinical procedures, such as coupling chlamydia tests with routine Pap testing, can sharply increase the proportion of sexually active young women screened. Increased prevention screening efforts are critical to preventing the serious health consequences of this infection, particularly infertility.

Recent studies have also shown that many young women who have been diagnosed with chlamydia may become re-infected by male partners who have not been diagnosed or treated. CDC's *2006 STD Treatment Guidelines* recommend that women be re-tested for chlamydia approximately three months after treatment, and also recommend the delivery of antibiotic therapy by heterosexual patients to their partners, if other strategies for reaching and treating partners are not likely to succeed. The availability of urine tests for chlamydia is likely contributing to increased detection of the disease in men, and consequently the rising rates of reported chlamydia among males in recent years [from 126.8 in 2002 to 173.0 in 2006].

Gonorrhea Is on the Rise

Gonorrhea is the second most commonly reported infectious disease in the United States, with 358,366 cases reported in 2006. Following a 74 percent decline in the rate of reported gonorrhea from 1975 through 1997, overall gonorrhea rates plateaued, then increased for the past two years. In 2006, the gonorrhea rate was 120.9 cases per 100,000 population, an increase of 5.5 percent since 2005

Shown is an electron micrograph scan of *Chlamydia trachomatis,* a bacteria that causes a variety of STDs, including chlamydia. **(Phototake Inc./Alamy)**

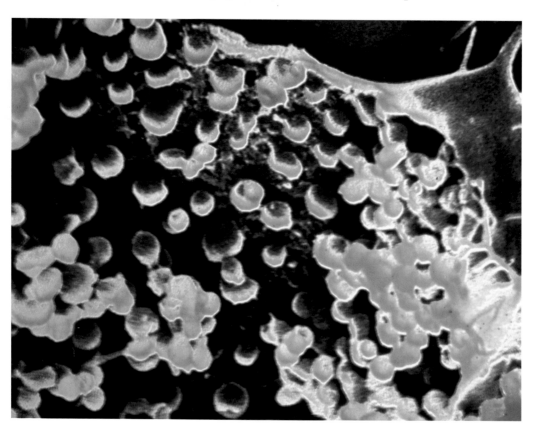

and an increase for the second consecutive year. Like chlamydia, gonorrhea is substantially under-diagnosed and under-reported, and approximately twice as many new infections are estimated to occur each year as are reported.

As in previous years, the South had the highest gonorrhea rate among the four regions of the country. Additionally, rates rose in the South for the first time in eight years, increasing 12.3 percent between 2005 and 2006 from 141.8 to 159.2 per 100,000 population.

While the impact is greatest in the South, researchers are also concerned about continued increases in the West, where the rate of reported gonorrhea cases rose 2.9 percent between 2005 and 2006 [from 80.5 to 82.8 per 100,000] and increased by 31.8 percent between 2002 and 2006.

Between 2002 and 2006, the rate in the South declined slightly [from 161.8 to 159.2], the Northeast declined 21.2 percent [from 93.6 to 73.8] and the rate in the Midwest showed minimal change [from 142.2 in 2002 to 136.9 in 2006].

Increased Drug Resistance Leads to New CDC Treatment Guidelines

Drug resistance is an increasingly important concern in the treatment and prevention of gonorrhea. CDC monitors trends in gonorrhea drug resistance through the Gonococcal Isolate Surveillance Project [GISP], which tests gonorrhea samples ["isolates"] from the first 25 men with urethral gonorrhea attending STD clinics each month in sentinel clinics across the United States [28 cities in 2006].

Overall, 13.8 percent of gonorrhea isolates tested through GISP in 2006 demonstrated resistance to fluoroquinolones, a leading class of antibiotics previously recommended to treat the disease, compared to 9.4 percent in 2005 and 6.8 percent in 2004. Resistance to the fluoroquinolones has been highest among men who have sex with men [MSM]. From 2005 to 2006, resistance among heterosexuals nearly doubled from 3.8 to 7 percent and continued to increase among MSM from 29 to 39 percent.

Syphilis Rebounds

The rate of primary and secondary [P&S] syphilis—the most infectious stages of the disease—decreased throughout the 1990s, and in 2000 reached an all-time low. However, over the past six years, the syphilis rate in the United States has been increasing. Between 2005 and 2006, the national P&S syphilis rate increased 13.8 percent, from 2.9 to 3.3 cases per 100,000 population, and the number of cases increased from 8,724 to 9,756.

The overall increase in syphilis rates from 2005 to 2006 was driven primarily by increases among males, with the rate increasing by 11.8 percent [from 5.1 per 100,000 population in 2005 to 5.7 in 2006] in that group. However, the rate among females increased for the second year in a row, following a decade of declines [from 0.9 per 100,000 in 2005 to 1.0 in 2006, an increase of 11.1 percent]. Additionally, the rate of congenital syphilis [i.e., transmission from mother to newborn] increased slightly in 2006 [from 8.2 per 100,000 live births in 2005 to 8.5 in 2006]. While it is too early to determine if the increase among newborns is a trend, increases in congenital syphilis have historically followed increases among women.

The rate of P&S syphilis among men has risen 54 percent over the past five years [from 3.7 per 100,000 in 2002 to 5.7 per 100,000 in 2006), driving overall increases in syphilis rates for the nation. Several sources of data suggest that increased transmission of P&S syphilis among MSM may be largely responsible for these increases. Over time, the disparity between male and female case rates has grown considerably. The P&S syphilis rate among males is now nearly six times the rate among females, whereas the rates were almost equivalent a decade ago.

African-American Women Are at Risk

While P&S syphilis rates remained substantially lower among females than males, overall rates among females increased

FAST FACT

Some STDs, such as herpes and human papillomavirus (HPV), are believed to be even more widespread than the top three reported by the CDC, but no national data is collected on them.

for the second year in a row, after a decade of declines, with an increase of 11.1 percent between 2005 and 2006 [from 0.9 to 1.0]. This increase was largely driven by increased rates among African-American females, which rose 11.4 percent [from 4.4 in 2005 to 4.9 in 2006]. Rates among females in all other racial/ethnic groups declined or remained stable.

The reasons for these overall increases among females are not yet clear. However, CDC is currently analyzing this trend to better understand the factors driving this increase.

Eliminating syphilis as a health threat in the United States will require an ongoing commitment to syphilis education, testing, and treatment in all populations affected. In May 2006, CDC released its updated National Plan to Eliminate Syphilis, designed to sustain elimination efforts in populations traditionally at risk, including African Americans and women of all races and ethnicities, and to support innovative solutions to fight the resurgence of syphilis among MSM.

The Human Immunodeficiency Virus (HIV) and How It Causes AIDS

Mohammad Said Maani Takrouri

Human Immunodeficiency Virus (HIV) is the deadliest of sexually transmitted diseases. It causes a fatal disease called Acquired Immune Deficiency Syndrome, or AIDS. Since its first detection in the early 1980s, AIDS has led to the deaths of an estimated 25 million people worldwide. In the following selection a doctor explains the disease, its spread and detection, and its symptoms and treatments. Dr. Mohammad Said Maani Takrouri is a professor of anesthesiology at the College of Medicine, King Saud University in Saudi Arabia.

Several reports published by international health agencies like the World Health Organization (WHO) and the United Nations agencies (UNFPA) conclude that AIDS is the leading cause of death in sub-Saharan Africa and the fourth biggest killer worldwide. Since the epidemic began more than 24 years ago at least 60 million people worldwide have been infected with the virus and currently more than 45 million people live with HIV. . . .

SOURCE: Mohammad Said Maani Takrouri, "Basic Facts About HIV and AIDS," *The Internet Journal of Health,* 2005. Reproduced by permission.

These reports warn that the rates of infection are rising fastest in Eastern Europe and Russia. In 2001, there were an estimated 250000 new infections in this region. Russia has seen a 15-fold increase in infections over the years. Most of these cases are related to illegal drug use.

Sub-Saharan Africa continues to be the worst affected area. The report says that AIDS killed 2.3 million people in 2001 and that there were 3.4 million new HIV infections. The region is the only one where more women than men are infected by the virus. More than 28 million people in the region currently live with HIV, a prevalence of 8%. Most of these people, the report says, do not know they have the virus.

The epidemic also "threatens human welfare, developmental progress, and social stability on an unprecedented scale." Hardest hit countries could lose 20% of their gross domestic product by 2020. Steep drops in life expectancies are now beginning to occur. If it were not for HIV and AIDS, the average life expectancy in sub-Saharan Africa would be 62 years; it currently stands at 47 years.

The report says that marked increases in rates of infection in Asia and the Pacific, which have some of the world's most populous countries, are also of "particular concern." Reported HIV infections in China rose by 67% in the first six months of 2001, compared with the previous year. India has a prevalence of about 1% representing an estimated 3.86 million people.

Human Immunodeficiency Virus (HIV)

The abbreviations HIV stands for the virus named "human immunodeficiency virus". HIV is a member of retroviruses that infect cells of the human immune system (mainly CD4 positive T cells and macrophages—key components of the cellular immune system), and destroy or impair their function. Infection with this virus results in the progressive depletion of the immune system, leading to "immune deficiency".

The immune system is considered deficient when it can no longer fulfill its role of fighting off infection and diseases. Immunodeficient people are much more vulnerable to a wide range of infections, most of which are very rare among people without immune deficiency. Diseases associated with severe immunodeficiency are known as "opportunistic infections", because they take advantage of a weakened immune system.

Acquired Immunodeficiency Syndrome (AIDS)

AIDS stands for "acquired immunodeficiency syndrome" and describes the collection of symptoms and infections associated with acquired deficiency of the immune system. Infection with HIV has been established as the underlying cause of AIDS. The level of HIV in the body and the appearance of certain infections are used as indicators that HIV infection has progressed to AIDS.

The Symptoms of HIV Infection

Most people infected with HIV do not know that they have become infected because no symptoms develop immediately after the initial infection. Some people have a glandular fever-like illness (with fever, rash, joint pains and enlarged lymph nodes), which can occur at the time of development of antibodies to HIV and usually takes place between six weeks and three months after an infection has occurred—this is called seroconversion. Despite the fact that HIV infection does not cause any initial symptoms, an HIV-infected person is highly infectious and can transmit the virus to another person. The only way to determine whether HIV is present in a person's body is by taking an HIV test.

HIV infection causes a gradual depletion and weakening of the immune system. This results in an increased susceptibility of the body to infections and can lead to the development of AIDS.

> **FAST FACT**
>
> Approximately 40,000 people in America become infected with HIV each year.

When Can We Say That a Person Does Have AIDS?

The term AIDS applies to the most advanced stages of HIV infection. The majority of people infected with HIV, if not treated, develop signs of AIDS within 8–10 years.

Medical Management of AIDS

AIDS is identified on the basis of certain infections, grouped by the WHO:

- Stage I HIV disease is asymptomatic [shows no symptoms] and not categorized as AIDS
- Stage II (includes minor mucocutaneous [mucous-membrane] manifestations and recurrent upper respiratory tract infections)
- Stage III (includes unexplained chronic diarrhea for longer than a month, severe bacterial infections and pulmonary tuberculosis) or
- Stage IV (includes Toxoplasmosis [parasitic infection] of the brain, Candidiasis [infection] of the esophagus, trachea, bronchi or lungs and Kaposi's Sarcoma [tumor]). HIV diseases are used as indicators of AIDS. Most of these conditions are opportunistic infections [OI] that can be treated easily in healthy [individuals].

The length of time taken by infected patient to show signs of the disease can vary widely between individuals. With a healthy lifestyle, the time between infection with HIV and becoming ill with AIDS can be 10–15 years, sometimes longer. Antiretroviral [ARV] therapy can slow down the progression of AIDS by decreasing viral load in an infected body.

There is no cure for HIV/AIDS. Progression of the disease can be slowed down but cannot be stopped completely. The right combination of antiretroviral drugs can slow down the damage that HIV causes to the immune system and delay the onset of AIDS.

The available treatment and care consist of a number of different elements, including voluntary counseling and testing (VCT), support for the prevention of onward transmission of HIV, follow-up counseling, advice on food and nutrition, treatment of STIs [sexually transmitted infections], management of nutritional effects, prevention and treatment of opportunistic infections (OIs), and the provision of antiretroviral drugs. They are used in the treatment of HIV infection.

Antiretroviral drugs work as follows: Inside an infected cell, HIV produces new copies of itself, which can then go on to infect other healthy cells within the body. The more cells HIV infects, the greater its impact on the immune system (immunodeficiency). Antiretroviral drugs slow down the replication and, therefore, the spread of the virus within the body, by interfering with its replication process in different ways.

Nucleoside Reverse Transcriptase Inhibitors. HIV needs an enzyme called reverse transcriptase to generate new copies of itself. This group of drugs inhibits reverse transcriptase by preventing the process that replicates the virus's genetic material.

Non-Nucleoside Reverse Transcriptase Inhibitors. This group of drugs also interferes with the replication of HIV by binding to the reverse transcriptase enzyme itself. This prevents the enzyme from working and stops the production of new virus particles in the infected cells.

Protease Inhibitors. Protease is a digestive enzyme that is needed in the replication of HIV to generate new virus particles. It breaks down proteins and enzymes in the infected cells, which can then go on to infect other cells. The protease inhibitors prevent this breakdown of proteins and therefore slow down the production of new virus particles.

Other drugs that inhibit other stages in the virus's cycle (such as entry of the virus and fusion with an uninfected cell) are currently being tested in clinical trials.

The use of ARVs in combinations of three or more drugs has been shown to dramatically reduce AIDS-related

In 1985 a blood test was developed to measure the ratio of antibodies to HIV. These antibodies are the body's immune system response to HIV. **(James Pozanik/ Time Life Pictures/Getty Images)**

illness and death. While not a cure for AIDS, combination ARV therapy has enabled HIV-positive people to live longer, healthier, more productive lives by reducing viraemia (the amount of HIV in the blood) and increasing the number of CD4+ cells (white blood cells that are central to the effective functioning of the immune system).

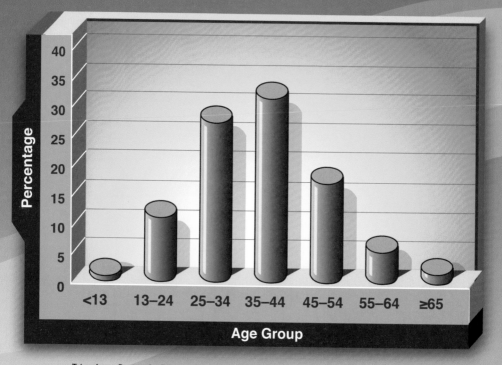

Age of Persons Diagnosed with HIV or AIDS in the United States in 2004

Taken from: Centers for Disease Control and Prevention, "HIV/AIDS Among Youth," June 2006.

For antiretroviral treatment to be effective for a long time, different antiretroviral drugs need to be combined. This is what is known as combination therapy. The term "Highly Active Anti-Retroviral Therapy" (HAART) is used to describe a combination of three or more anti-HIV drugs.

If one drug is taken on its own, it has been found that, over a period of time, changes in the virus enable it to build up resistance to the drug. The drug is then no longer effective and the virus starts to reproduce to the same extent as before. If two or more antiretroviral drugs are taken together, the rate at which resistance develops can be reduced substantially. Usually, the combination consists of two drugs that inhibit the reverse transcriptase enzyme and one protease.

Antiretroviral drugs should only be taken under medical supervision.

In developing countries, only about 5% of needy patients are receiving anti-retrovirals, while there is near universal access in high-income countries. The high cost of the medicines, inadequate health care infrastructure and lack of financing has prevented wide use of combination ARV treatment in low- and middle-income countries.

Twelve ARV medicines have been included in the WHO Essential Medicines List. The long-sought inclusion of ARVs in WHO's Essential Medicines List will encourage governments in hard-hit countries to further expand the distribution of these vital drugs to those who need them. Also, increased political and economic commitment in recent years, stimulated by people living with HIV/AIDS, civil society and other partners, has opened the scope for dramatic expansion of access to HIV therapy.

What Kind of Care Is Available When ARVs Are Not Accessible?

Other elements of care can help maintain a high quality of life when ARVs are not available. These include adequate nutrition, counseling, prevention and treatment of opportunistic infections and generally staying healthy.

Post-exposure preventive (PEP) treatment consists of medication, laboratory tests and counseling. PEP treatment must be initiated within hours of possible HIV exposure and must continue for a period of approximately four weeks. PEP treatment has not been proven to prevent the transmission of HIV. However, research studies suggest that, if the medication is initiated quickly after possible HIV exposure (ideally within two hours and not later than 72 hours following such exposure), it may be beneficial in preventing HIV infection.

Drug-Resistant Gonorrhea Is on the Rise

Rob Stein

Gonorrhea is a sexually transmitted disease caused by a rapidly repro-ducing bacterium. The standard treatment is a course of antibiotics, but as the following selection explains, the bacterium that causes gonorrhea is developing resistance to the medicines that until now have eradi-cated it. Resistance refers to the ability of bacteria to evolve defenses against antibiotics through random mutation and gene-swapping. In the following viewpoint journalist Rob Stein reports that resistant strains of the gonorrhea bacterium have proliferated in recent years. The federal Centers for Disease Control and Prevention (CDC) have declared one class of antibiotics off-limits due to high rates of resistance, and CDC experts are openly concerned that the remaining types may also lose their effectiveness. The problem, according to Stein, stems from overuse of antibiotics even in situations where they have no application, such as viral infections. If one kind of bacteria develops resistance, it can pass the trick on to another species through gene-swapping, scientists have learned. Rob Stein is a reporter for the *Washington Post*. He often reports on science and medicine.

SOURCE: Rob Stein, "Drugs Losing Efficacy Against Gonorrhea," *The Washington Post,* April 13, 2007. Copyright © 2007 The Washington Post Company. Reprinted with permission.

Antibiotic-resistant gonorrhea is spreading rapidly across the United States, federal health officials reported [in April 2007], raising alarm about doctors' ability to treat the common sexually transmitted infection.

New data from 26 U.S. cities show the number of resistant gonorrhea cases is rising dramatically, jumping from less than 1 percent of all gonorrhea cases to more than 13 percent in less than five years, the Atlanta-based Centers for Disease Control and Prevention [CDC] reported.

In response, the CDC advised doctors treating gonorrhea to immediately stop using ciprofloxacin, marketed as Cipro, and other antibiotics in its class, which have been the first line of defense against the disease, and resort to an older class of drugs to ensure patients are cured and do not spread the stubborn infection.

"We've lost the ability to use what had been the most reliable class of antibiotics," said John M. Douglas Jr., who heads the CDC's division of sexually transmitted disease prevention. "This is necessary to protect both public and private health."

Last Line of Defense

The development is alarming, Douglas and other experts said, because gonorrhea tends to develop resistance to antibiotics quickly, and doctors will be powerless to treat it if that happens with the remaining class of drugs. "We still have one effective class, but now it's the only one we've got," Douglas said. "This raises the possibility that we may slip into a situation where we have no highly reliable remedies."

The emergence of resistant gonorrhea marks the latest common pathogen to have shifted from an easily treated infection to a resistant form that is suddenly far more dangerous. "Gonorrhea has now joined the list of other superbugs for which treatment options have become dangerously few," said Henry Masur, president of the Infectious Disease Society of America.

Gonorrhea's resistance was probably caused by the same problem that led to resistance of other organisms—the casual use of antibiotics in the United States and overseas, which causes pathogens to mutate, Douglas and others said. "People will take these drugs for many reasons, like if they just have a cold, stimulating resistance to bacteria they don't know they have," Douglas said.

The emergence of resistant gonorrhea and other disease-causing agents comes as efforts to develop new antibiotics are flagging because of a lack of interest by the pharmaceutical industry, he noted. "We'll have a major problem on our hands if we don't develop new antibiotics," Douglas said.

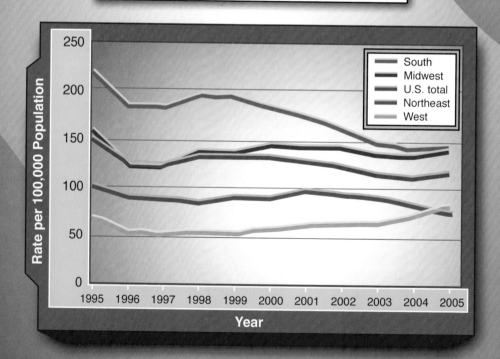

Gonorrhea Rates in the United States, 1995–2005

Taken from: Centers for Disease Control and Prevention, "Erratum," March 22, 2007.

A Halt for One Drug

Gonorrhea is the second-most-common sexually transmitted disease in the United States after chlamydia, infecting more than 700,000 Americans each year. The highest reported rates occur among sexually active teenagers, young adults and African Americans. If untreated, the disease—which usually does not produce symptoms until the later stages—can lead to sterility and potentially life-threatening complications.

Resistant strains of the bacteria that cause gonorrhea were first detected in Asia. Resistant gonorrhea then apparently spread to Hawaii and California, before emerging elsewhere around the United States, first among gay men. In response, the CDC recommended doctors stop using Cipro and other drugs in its class, known as fluoroquinolones, to treat gonorrhea in California and Hawaii, and among gay men nationwide.

> **FAST FACT**
>
> In recent years the West Coast and surrounding states have experienced a swift rise in gonorrhea. From 2000 to 2005, the rate of gonorrhea infection in the western states increased 42 percent to 81.5 cases per 100,000 population.

The agency expanded that recommendation to everyone nationwide after detecting a sharp rise in resistant gonorrhea among heterosexual males. The rate increased from 0.6 percent of all cases in 2001 to 6.7 percent in the first half of 2006—an 11-fold increase. The resistance appears to be widespread around the country, with particularly sharp increases occurring in some cities. In Philadelphia, the rate jumped from 1.2 to 26.6 percent. In Miami, it increased from 2.1 percent to 15.3 percent. At the same time the rate continued to rise rapidly among gay men, increasing from 1.6 percent to 38 percent of all cases.

The news comes as the rate of new gonorrhea infections has started rising in some Western states. Public health experts warned that the recommendation to change the standard care will make it more difficult to stem the spread of the disease because the main weapon is to diagnose and treat patients quickly before they can infect someone else.

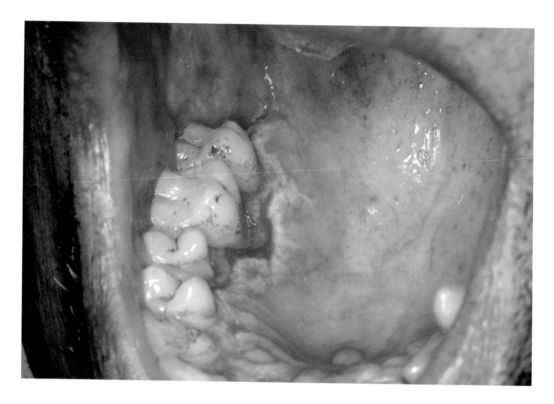

A gonorrhea lesion is shown growing in a patient's mouth. Resistant gonorrhea is on the rise among young heterosexual males in the United States. (Medical-on-Line/ Alamy)

Shots May Help

The CDC is recommending doctors use a class of antibiotics known as cephalosporins, in particular the drug ceftriaxone, which is given by injection, making its use more painful and complicated. Many doctors do not typically stock the shots. And patients who are allergic to penicillin often cannot use the drugs.

While significant resistance to cephalosporins has not been detected, the agency is working with state and local health departments, as well as the World Health Organization, to monitor the possible emergence of resistance to that class.

Chlamydia Has Become a Leading Cause of Infertility in Women

Jill Turner

Chlamydia is a sexually transmitted disease that hits women especially hard. It is the leading cause of infertility in both America and Western Europe. In the following viewpoint British writer Jill Turner describes the dangers of chlamydia for both women and men. The bacterial disease is on the rise, in part because it is easily transmitted and often presents no symptoms. The effects of chlamydia can be devastating. According to Turner, infertility commonly results in women and may be occurring in men as well as a result of infection with chlamydia. The disease strikes most often among young people, making the consequences especially tragic. Even babies developing in the womb may suffer harm from their mother's infection, according to Turner. She recommends that anyone who has had sex without a condom be tested for the disease. Experts say that chlamydia can be spread even when condoms are used, because it can survive on the skin near the genitals. Testing, therefore, may be a good choice for any sexually active teen. Jill Turner writes on health and lifestyle for the *Manchester Evening News* in northern England.

SOURCE: Jill Turner, "Chlamydia: The Hidden Danger," *Manchester Evening News*, November 13, 2007. Copyright © 2007 Manchester Evening News Media. Reproduced by permission.

I t is the single largest cause of fertility problems in Western Europe, yet most people don't even know what it is—or that they may be infected.

Chlamydia, known as the 'silent epidemic' for this reason, is the most common sexually transmitted infection (STI)—with the number of people infected tripling since the 1990s. Last year, 113,585 cases were reported in the UK.

And while it is known to damage the fallopian tubes that carry the egg to the womb in females, hindering chances of future pregnancy and childbirth, doctors have also discovered that it can attack sperm in infected men, and could be a cause of decreased male fertility.

Which is why the British Health Protection Agency last week [November 2007] launched a national campaign to get more men screened for the disease. Now colleges, youth clubs and prisons will offer screening with free kits available online.

Men Fear Seeking Help

Pharmacist Angela Chalmers is certainly seeing more and more cases.

"It worries me how little people know about chlamydia," she says. I am particularly concerned about the ignorance of young men who appear not to want to come forward. I think they're worried about the embarrassment, or they see it as somehow macho not to bother, or they just don't see it as a problem for them, but it is, and it can be a serious one.

In this country we are always being told that male fertility is dropping and I am sure that this is a big contributing factor. And, if that is not enough, in extreme cases, where chlamydia has been left untreated, it can even start to affect the eyesight or pass such problems to unborn children.

Most people don't display any symptoms, which is why so many cases go untreated. Those that can occur include pain when urinating, unusual discharge and, for women, bleeding after sex or between periods.

A Danger to Pregnancy

If untreated, up to 40 percent of women sufferers can develop pelvic inflammatory disease, which causes tubal scarring [scaring of the fallopian tubes], leading to infertility and an increased risk of ectopic [outside the womb] pregnancy.

In men, chlamydia is also the most common cause of inflammation in the testicles and sperm conducting tubes, leading to pain and swelling of the scrotum.

At its worst, it can also cause infections in the eye, which can lead to permanent visual impairment. Pregnant women who are carrying the infection can pass it to their unborn child and give them lung and eye infections.

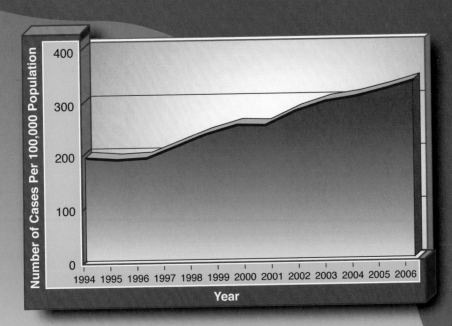

Chlamydia Rates Are on the Rise in the United States

Taken from: Utah Department of Health, "Rates of Reported Chlamydia Cases by Year, Utah and U.S., 1994–2006," August 23, 2007.

Chlamydia is most common and most likely to cause serious complications in young women. If you are female, under-25 and sexually active, you have a one-in-10 chance of having it. The risk is even higher if you are under 20 and having unprotected sex. The risk age for males is between 16 and 30.

Latest figures show women aged 16 to 19 as the biggest group infected, with 1,337 per 100,000 tested diagnosed with chlamydia, followed by men aged 20 to 24, with 1,144 per 100,000 diagnosed. . . .

Tests Are Key

The sad fact is that chlamydia is preventable, by having protected sex, and treatable, although for some women by the time they get treatment it may well be too late to halt long-term fertility problems.

> **FAST FACT**
>
> Contrary to popular myth, young people cannot avoid chlamydia by engaging in oral sex. The bacteria can infect the throat via oral sexual contact with an infected partner.

Doctors advise being tested for the STI whether you are presenting symptoms or not. Basically, if you have ever had sex without using a condom, you are at risk.

And there is no correlation between promiscuous behaviour or the number of partners you have had. You only need to have unprotected sex with one person who happens to have the infection to get chlamydia.

Chalmers, who works for Boots [health and beauty retailer] says: "It is frightening to think this, but if you have unprotected sex with one person, you are sleeping with the sexual history of all the partners they have had unprotected sex with, and all the partners they have had unprotected sex with as well, and so on.

"You can be playing Russian Roulette with your sexual health, with thousands of strangers."

The infection can also stay unrecognised for months, if not years, so if you do find you are infected you should encourage ex-partners to get tested as well.

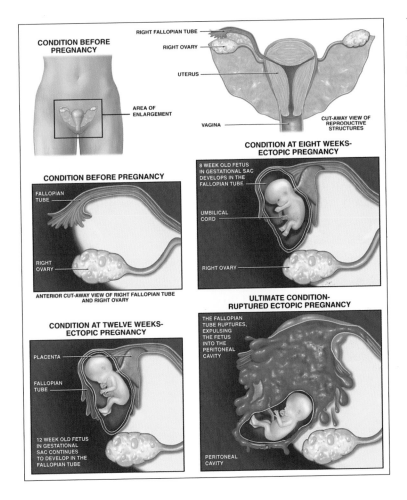

The chronological progression of an ectopic pregnancy is shown in this diagram. If left untreated, it can lead to tubal scarring and infertility. (**Nucleus Medical Art, Inc.**/Alamy)

Adds Chalmers:

A woman I know was in a monogamous relationship with a man who was her only partner.

One day she collapsed at work with pelvic inflammatory disease, which had developed because she had contracted chlamydia from him.

He had only had one other sexual relationship, but—unaware to him—had chlamydia.

Eight years later, they are still struggling to start a family. They've said to me: "If only we'd known, we could have prevented all this." It's a very sad situation.

Urine Sample Works

In the past, a chlamydia test for women was similar to a smear test, but now both men and women can provide urine samples to get the all-clear. However, it can take up to two weeks after unprotected sex for any infection to show up.

Apart from going to your GP [general practitioner], there are many other places to get tested, and treatment is by antibiotics. . . . Both partners should be treated; repeated infection can cause far worse fertility problems for women.

However, although with men antibiotics will clear up the problem, in women internal damage may already be done, even after the chlamydia has cleared up.

Chalmers warns: "Chlamydia can wreck your chances of having a family and other people's as well. It's really not fair to yourself or others not to get tested and not to have protected sex. Just use a condom. The repercussions—for more than just you—are far worse."

Herpes Often Makes Its Way from Victim to Victim by Stealth

National Institute of Allergy and Infectious Diseases

Herpes is one of a number of sexually transmitted diseases that are caused by viruses. That means antibiotics are useless for treating them. Viral diseases can only be prevented or managed, not cured. In the following article the National Institute of Allergy and Infectious Diseases describes how herpes is transmitted, what its symptoms are, and what steps can be taken to avoid or manage the disease. Unfortunately, according to the authors, many people contract the disease without any warning, because they have unprotected sex with someone who has herpes but no symptoms of the disease. The infected partner may not even know he or she has the disease. However, a lack of symptoms does not guarantee a lack of consequences, which may include greater susceptibility to the virus that causes AIDS. The National Institute of Allergy and Infectious Diseases is a federal agency that conducts and supports research to better understand, treat, and ultimately prevent infectious, immunologic, and allergic diseases.

SOURCE: National Institute of Allergy and Infectious Diseases, "Genital Herpes," in National Institutes of Health, November 30, 2007.

Genital herpes is a sexually transmitted infection (STI). According to the Centers for Disease Control and Prevention (CDC), 1 out of 5 American teenagers and adults is infected with genital herpes. Women are more commonly infected than men. In the United States, 1 out of 4 women has herpes.

Although at least 45 million people in the United States have genital herpes infection, there has been a substantial decrease in cases from 21 percent to 17 percent, according to a 1999 to 2004 CDC survey. Much of the decrease was in the 14 to 19 year age group, and continued through the young adult group.

Genital herpes is caused by herpes simplex virus (HSV). There are two types of HSV.

- HSV type 1 most commonly infects the mouth and lips, causing sores known as fever blisters or cold sores.

- HSV type 2 is the usual cause of genital herpes, but it also can infect the mouth.

Silent Contagion

If you have genital herpes infection, you can easily pass or transmit the virus to an uninfected partner during sex.

Most people get genital herpes by having sex with someone who is shedding the herpes virus either during an outbreak or an asymptomatic (without symptoms) period. People who do not know they have herpes play an important role in transmission because they are unaware they can infect a sexual partner.

You can transmit herpes through close contact other than sexual intercourse, through oral sex or close skin-to-skin contact, for example. The virus is spread rarely, if at all, by objects such as a toilet seat or hot tub.

People with herpes should follow a few simple steps to avoid spreading the infection to other places on their body or other people.

- Avoid touching the infected area during an outbreak, and wash your hands after contact with that area.

- Do not have sexual contact (vaginal, oral, or anal) from the time of your first genital symptoms until your symptoms are completely gone.

What to Look For

Symptoms of herpes are called outbreaks. The first outbreak appears within 2 weeks after you become infected and can last for several weeks. These symptoms might include tingling or sores (lesions) near the area where the virus has entered your body, such as on your genital or rectal area, on your buttocks or thighs. Occasionally, these sores may appear on other parts of your body where the virus

Infected but Unaware: Herpes Simplex Virus Type 2

20% of people infected with herpes simplex virus type two (HSV-2) have no symptoms at all.

60% of people infected with HSV-2 have symptoms but do not know they are infected with the virus.

20% of people infected with HSV-2 have symptoms and know they are infected with the virus.

Taken from: Herpesnet, "How Common Is Herpes?" www.herpesweb.net.

has entered through broken skin. Sores also can appear inside the vagina and on the cervix (opening to the womb) in women, or in the urinary passage of women and men. Small red bumps appear first, develop into small blisters, and then become itchy, painful sores that might develop a crust and will heal without leaving a scar.

Sometimes, there is a crack or raw area or some redness without pain, itching, or tingling. Other symptoms that may accompany the first (and less often future) outbreak of genital herpes are fever, headache, muscle aches, painful or difficult urination, vaginal discharge, and swollen glands in the groin area.

Often, though, people don't recognize their first or subsequent outbreaks. People who have mild or no symptoms at all may not think they are infected with herpes. They can still transmit the virus to others, however.

Infected for Life

In most people, the virus can become active and cause outbreaks several times a year. This is called a recurrence, and infected people can have symptoms. HSV remains in certain nerve cells of your body for life. When the virus is triggered to be active, it travels along the nerves to your skin. There, it makes more virus and sometimes new sores near the site of the first outbreak. Recurrences are generally much milder than the first outbreak of genital herpes. HSV-2 genital infection is more likely to result in recurrences than HSV-1 genital infection. Recurrences become less common over time.

Symptoms from recurrences might include itching, tingling, vaginal discharge, and a burning feeling or pain in the genital or anal area. Sores may be present during a recurrence, but sometimes they are small and easily overlooked.

Sometimes, the virus can become active but not cause any visible sores or any symptoms. During these times, small amounts of the virus may be shed at or near places of the first infection, in fluids from the mouth, penis, or vagina, or from barely noticeable sores. This is called asymptomatic shedding. Even though you are not aware of the shedding, you can infect a sexual partner during this time. Asymptomatic shedding is an important factor in the spread of herpes.

Diagnosing Herpes

Your health care provider can diagnose typical genital herpes by looking at the sores. Some cases, however, are more difficult to diagnose.

The virus sometimes, but not always, can be detected by a laboratory test called a culture. A culture is done when your health care provider uses a swab to get and study material from a suspected herpes sore. You may still have genital herpes, however, even if your culture is negative (which means it does not show HSV).

A blood test called type-specific test can tell whether you are infected with HSV-1 or HSV-2. The type-specific test results plus the location of the sores will help your health care provider to find out whether you have genital infection.

A diagnosis of genital herpes can have substantial emotional effects on you and your sexual partner, whether or not you have symptoms. Proper counseling and treatment can help you and your partner learn to cope with the disease, recurrent episodes, personal relationships, and fertility issues.

FAST FACT

A woman who acquires genital herpes before becoming pregnant has a relatively low risk of passing the virus to her baby, but a woman who contracts genital herpes during pregnancy—especially late in the pregnancy—has a higher risk of passing the virus to the baby.

Treatments and Precautions

Although there is no cure for genital herpes, your health care provider might prescribe an antiviral medicine to treat your symptoms and to help prevent future outbreaks. This can decrease the risk of passing herpes to sexual partners. Medicines to treat genital herpes are:

- Acyclovir (Zovirax)
- Famciclovir (Famvir)
- Valacyclovir (Valtrex) . . .

Symptoms of herpes are shown on a man's shoulder. Small red bumps appear first and develop into blisters that are itchy and painful. (**Scott Camazine**/Alamy)

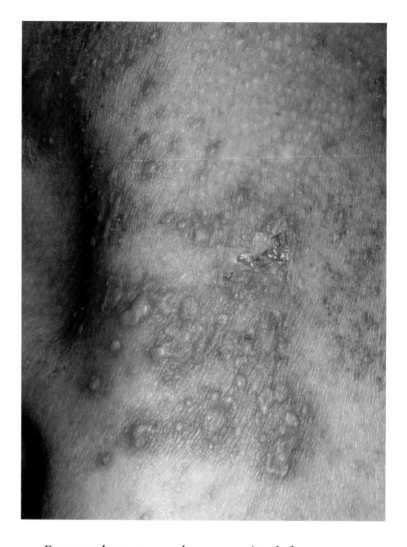

Because herpes can be transmitted from someone who has no symptoms, using the precautions listed below is not enough to prevent transmission. Recently, the Food and Drug Administration approved Valtrex for use in preventing transmission of genital herpes. It has to be taken continuously by the infected person, and while it significantly decreases the risk of the transmission of herpes, transmission can still occur.

Do not have oral-genital contact if you or your sexual partner has any symptoms or findings of oral herpes.

Using barriers such as latex condoms during sexual activity may decrease transmission when you use them consistently and correctly, but transmission can still occur since condoms may not cover all infected areas.

You can get tested to find out if you are infected with the herpes virus.

Effects on Health

Genital herpes infections usually do not cause serious health problems in healthy adults. In some people whose immune systems do not work properly, however, genital herpes outbreaks can be unusually severe and long lasting.

Occasionally, people with normal immune systems can get herpes infection of the eye, called ocular herpes. Ocular herpes is usually caused by HSV-1 but sometimes by HSV-2. It can occasionally result in serious eye disease, including blindness.

A woman with herpes who is pregnant can pass the infection to her baby. A baby born with herpes might die or have serious brain, skin, or eye problems. Pregnant women who have herpes, or whose sex partner has herpes should discuss the situation with her health care provider. Together they can make a plan to reduce her or her baby's risk of getting infected. Babies who are born with herpes do better if the disease is recognized and treated early.

Genital herpes, like other genital diseases that cause sores, is important in the spread of HIV infection. A person infected with herpes may have a greater risk of getting HIV. This may be due to the open sores caused by the herpes infection or by other factors in the immune system. In addition, HIV-positive people may be more contagious for herpes.

Research

The National Institute of Allergy and Infectious Diseases (NIAID) supports research on genital herpes and HSV. Studies are currently underway to develop better treatments for the millions of people who suffer from genital herpes. While some scientists are carrying out clinical trials to determine the best way to use existing medicines, others are studying the biology of HSV. NIAID scientists have identified certain genes and enzymes (proteins) that the virus needs to survive. They are hopeful that drugs aimed at disrupting these viral targets might lead to the design of more effective treatments.

Meanwhile, other researchers are devising methods to control the virus' spread. Two important means of preventing HSV infection are vaccines and topical microbicides [germ-killing gels or foams].

Several different vaccines are in various stages of development. These include vaccines made from proteins on the HSV cell surface, peptides or chains of amino acids, and the DNA of the virus itself. NIAID and GlaxoSmithKline are supporting a large clinical trial in women of an experimental vaccine that may help prevent transmission of genital herpes. The Herpevac Trial is being conducted at more than 50 sites in the U.S. and Canada.

CHAPTER 2

Controversies About Sexually Transmitted Diseases

Use of Condoms to Prevent STDs Is Unjustifiable

John B. Shea

Condoms are the most widely recommended barrier protection against the spread of sexually transmitted diseases. However, their use is controversial. Opposition is strongest from Catholic authorities. In the following viewpoint physician John B. Shea explains the Catholic view of morality as it relates to contraception in general and condoms in particular. He quotes extensively from Monsignor Vincent Foy, a retired priest who has written that "the greatest enemy of the Church's missionary activity is not the world around her, but the deep internal wound of the contraceptive mentality." In addition to arguing that condoms are immoral (because they block conception), Shea insists that they are unreliable in preventing the transmission of the virus that causes AIDS. Shea is a retired physician who writes frequently on conservative Catholic perspectives on sexuality and reproduction. He lives in Toronto.

Photo on previous page. Although condoms are the most widely used barrier protection against STDs, their use remains controversial. (Frances M. Roberts/Alamy)

Father Michael Stogre S.J., in an article on AIDS in *The Catholic Register*, May 22, 2005, stated, "Currently, when a spouse has AIDS, the use of condoms to prevent transmission of the virus is more and

SOURCE: John B. Shea, "Why Do Some Clergy Question Abstinence in the Fight Against HIV/AIDS?" *Catholic Insight*, October 2005. Copyright 2005 *Catholic Insight*. Reproduced by permission.

more being seen not as a contraceptive measure, but as a justifiable medical intervention."

Support for the use of condoms to prevent the spread of HIV/AIDS has recently come from some surprising sources—cardinals, individual bishops and Catholic bishops' conferences. Since 2004, support has been expressed by the bishops' conferences of Spain, Mexico, and England and Wales (through its agency, the Catholic Agency for Overseas Development). The French bishops expressed their support in 1996. Supporting cardinals included [Cormac] Murphy-O'Connor (Westminster, England), [Godfried] Daneels (Brussels, Belgium), [Javier Lozano] Barragan (President of the Pontifical Council for Health Care Workers), and [Georges] Cottier (household theologian to Pope John Paul II). Supporting bishops are Kevin Dowling (South Africa), and Fabian Marulauda (Colombia). The Spanish bishops' subsequent clarification said that responsible and moral sexual activity is the only "advisable" way to avoid disease. The statement stopped short of the Catholic teaching that sexual abstinence and faithfulness in marriage are the only morally permissible means of avoiding disease. One is forced to ask the question whether this clerical support is morally correct and based on sound medical science?

Tenets of Catholic Morality

The nature of an act (its *object*) determines its morality. Intercourse with a condom is intrinsically disordered, evil in and of itself.

The intention of the acting person is important, but it cannot change the nature of the act of intercourse with a condom. It remains an intrinsic evil.

The reason why a good intention is not in itself sufficient, but a correct choice of actions is needed, is that the human act depends on its object, whether that object is capable or not of being ordered to God, thus bringing about the perfection of the person [as written in *Veritatis*

Splendor]. "Reason attests that there are objects of the human act which are by their nature incapable of being ordered to God, because they radically contradict the good of the person made in His image. These are the acts which, in the Church's moral tradition, have been termed 'intrinsically evil' (*intrinsece malum*) on account of their very object, and quite apart from ulterior intentions of the one acting and the circumstances.

The law of "double effect" requires that if an action has two effects, the action itself must be morally good or indifferent. Since intercourse with a condom is intrinsically evil, the law of double effect does not apply.

[As written in *Humanae Vitae:*] "Though it is true that sometimes it is lawful to tolerate a lesser evil to avoid a greater moral evil or in order to promote a greater moral good, it is never lawful, even for the gravest reasons, to do evil that good may come of it." When comparing greater or lesser evils, the comparison must be between evils of a similar nature. Risk of disease is a physical and not a moral evil, whereas intercourse with a condom is a moral evil. Some theologians hold that the risk of HIV infection is more evil than the use of a condom to reduce that risk. This statement is not doctrinally sound.

To advise or suggest evil is to induce evil and that is always a scandal.

The Use of Condoms Is a Moral Evil

[Retired priest Monsignor] Vincent Foy of Toronto states that in considering the question of the lesser evil, some distinctions must be made between homosexual intercourse and heterosexual intercourse and also between intrinsic and extrinsic factors.

> Homosexual intercourse: it is true that, intrinsically, homosexual intercourse with or without a condom are equivalent moral evils, even though they are not precisely

FAST FACT

The archbishop of the Catholic Church in Mozambique, Francisco Chimoio, has claimed that condoms sent to that African nation from Europe are deliberately infected with HIV.

the same act. In both there is sodomitical intent. Extrinsically, sodomy with or without a condom is not a moral equivalent. A condom must be obtained and obtaining a condom for sex is a moral evil, both in itself and by support of the condom industry. Obtaining a condom may or may not give scandal. Obtaining a condom makes the sin of sodomy more likely and its repetition more probable. Repetition can lead to a habit of perversion and greater likelihood of loss of faith and damnation. It also

Condom Use Among Young Africans

The following graph shows the percentage of young people (15–24-year-olds) in selected sub-Saharan African countries who report using a condom at last sex with a nonmarital noncohabiting partner (of those who have had sex with such a partner in the last 12 months).

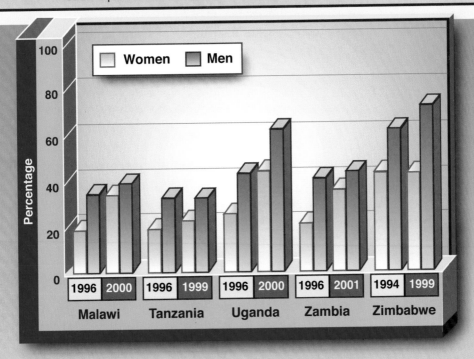

Taken from: UNAIDS, "Bringing Comprehensive HIV Prevention to Scale," 2004.

leads to greater danger of the physical evil called AIDS. When one is told that condom use is the lesser evil, the advice may be perceived as undue toleration of evil and neglect of proper spiritual direction.

Heterosexual intercourse: In heterosexual intercourse, and that means 95% of intercourse, the moral evil of using a condom is greater both intrinsically and extrinsically.

Intrinsically the act is transformed from a natural one to an unnatural one even when contraception does not take place. Even spouses who are sterile may not use a condom to protect themselves from infection because the inherent unity and procreative nature of the conjugal act is destroyed. It becomes an act of mutual self-abuse. Intrinsically, there is a greater moral evil when the condom acts as a contraceptive. Contraception is an intrinsic evil and immoral whether in or out of marriage.

Extrinsically, condom use brings its own train of evils. There is the act of obtaining or receiving a condom. Condom possession may be a constant temptation to sin as well as an instrument of seduction. It may lead to a habit of fornication and a contraceptive mentality that may destroy a future marriage. Another extrinsic possibility is the multiplication of malefactors, not only condom manufacturers and vendors, but school boards, or trustees, or teachers, or counselors, or chaplains, who advise condom use, or neglect the spiritual direction needed by the young. So in heterosexual intercourse, there are both intrinsic and extrinsic reasons to say that to use a condom is never the lesser sin. It is clear that support for the use of the condom to prevent spread of HIV is in contradiction to Church teaching.

Doubts About Condoms' Efficacy

The National Institutes of Health in 2001 investigated the world scientific literature relating to the ability of condom use to reduce the risk of the transmission of sex-

ually transmitted disease. The NIH in 2001, found that the consistent and correct use of the condom reduced the risk of HIV transmission by 85%. A 15% risk remained. A more recent study, in 2003, concluded that consistent use of the condom results in only 80% reduction in HIV transmission. Other circumstances such as rupture of a condom increase the risk. Liviana Calzavera Ph.D., an epidemiologist at the University of Toronto, Faculty of Medicine, has stated that imperfect condom use probably offers as high a risk of transmitting HIV as does intercourse without the use of the condom.

A key question remains. Does distribution of condoms lessen the spread or increase the transmission of HIV/AIDS? Dr. George Mulcaire-Jones, president and founder of Maternal Life International, who knows firsthand that condoms don't work because of his regular travels to Africa to work hands-on in the war against AIDS, says that condoms do little physically to prevent transmission of

Pope Benedict XVI spoke in November 2005 in St. Peter's Square about AIDS victims and the need to cure the disease, but avoided the issue of the Church's ban on condoms. (Max Rossi/ Reuters/Landov)

HIV and exacerbate the problem by promoting promiscuity where that behaviour is most deadly, Asia and Africa. Norman Hearst, professor at University of California and Sanny Chen, an epidemiologist at the South Africa Health Department state that in many sub-Saharan African countries, high HIV transmission rates have continued despite high condom use. They also said that no clear examples have emerged yet of a country that has turned back a generalized epidemic primarily by means of condom prevention, adding that the main cause of the falling incidence of HIV in Uganda was a substantial drop in the numbers of casual sexual partners and that measuring condom efficacy is nearly impossible. Botswana, Zimbabwe, Kenya, and South Africa have the highest rates of HIV and also the highest availability of condoms.

One more question. Is it reasonable to recommend the use of the condom to a married couple where one partner has HIV infection? The condom does not abolish the risk of transmitting this horrible and ultimately fatal disease. Intercourse puts the uninfected spouse at great risk. There is therefore a doubt about taking the life of an innocent human being, a *dubium facti*, which as such, creates the same obligation as certainty. Self-sacrifice and abstinence are the only valid moral options.

Use of Condoms to Prevent STDs Is Justified

James Carroll

The Catholic Church's opposition to the use of condoms has engendered much criticism, not least from within the church itself. In the following selection, a newspaper columnist who is himself a Catholic deems the church's position on the use of condoms to prevent the transmission of HIV a mistake of catastrophic proportions. James Carroll, who attended seminary and served as a Catholic chaplain for five years, castigates the church hierarchy for its "rigid adherence" to the prohibition on condoms despite the deadly consequences. Millions in Africa and elsewhere have been needlessly infected, Carroll says, because the church's influence has prevented the use of condoms. Such a stance runs contrary to the church's historical commitment to medical service as an act of mercy. An announcement by the pope that the church will reexamine its position on the use of condoms to prevent the spread of AIDS is a welcome step in the right direction, he says. A novelist and playwright, Carroll remains a Catholic. His column has appeared regularly in the *Boston Globe* since 1992.

SOURCE: James Carroll, "Outlawed AIDS Prevention," *The Boston Globe*, May 1, 2006. Copyright © 2006 Globe Newspaper Company. Reproduced by permission of the author.

Caring for the sick has always been a defining act of religion, as if every conception of God must be measured by its generation or compassion. Among Catholics, the tradition of the "corporal works of mercy," associated with Jesus himself, long ago spawned a commitment to provide for the health of human beings, which led to the institutionalization of medical service. Catholic hospitals are the pride of the church. When I was a child, family illness prompted visits to Providence Hospital in Washington, and I remember the winged garb of the nursing sisters as a particular symbol of all that made life on this earth trustworthy.

Such associations form the backdrop of the shock it was when the Catholic Church failed in its response to the arrival of HIV/AIDS. Not that compassion was lacking. Catholic hospitals and other ministries threw themselves into caring for those who became infected, and today, across Europe, Africa, and the Americas, much of such care is provided in Catholic settings. But the urgent need for active prevention soon showed itself, and because the disease can be transmitted sexually, that required the advocacy of condom use.

Thwarting the Surgeon General

In 1987 US Surgeon General C. Everett Koop recommended condoms for the prevention of the spread of HIV. One scientific study after another demonstrated the effectiveness of condoms in reducing risk of infection, yet centers of cultural conservatism resisted that message—none more consistently than the hierarchy of the Catholic Church.

"Although proven strategies exist to prevent new HIV infections," the UN declared in 2005, "essential prevention strategies reach only a fraction of those who need them." The Vatican has a special responsibility here, for it not only repeatedly rejected condom use for the sake of HIV prevention, but argue—for example in its 2003 document "Family Values and Safe Sex—that condoms, instead of inhibiting the spread of HIV/AIDS, promote it. This unconscionable denial was rooted in the most rigid of moral theologies, as if any loosening of Vatican condemnations of contraception—never mind that disease prevention differs from birth control—would lead to the collapse of Catholic authority.

In the years since Koop's advocacy of condoms, HIV/AIDS has continued to spread, so that by now more than 40 million people are infected, and the rates are going up (13,000 new infections each day). No Vatican policy could have stopped the spread of the disease, but there can be no doubt that Vatican rejection of condoms, and its aggressive campaign against condom use, helped that spread, especially in areas of the world where Catholic influence is high.

In 1987 U.S. Surgeon General C. Everett Koop first recommended the use of condoms to help prevent the spread of HIV. (Terry Ashe/Time Life Pictures/Getty Images)

A Reconsideration in the Works

Last week [April 2007] came news reports that Pope Benedict XVI has ordered a Vatican reconsideration of its position on condoms and HIV/AIDS. "We are conducting a very profound scientific, technical, and moral study," said the head of the Vatican office for healthcare. The study may be restricted to condom use between married couples, one of whom carries the infection, but even a change in that limited context would be significant. Any mitigation of absolutism in Vatican rejection of condoms would be a welcome step in the right direction. Indeed, the announcement that a change is being considered is already a mitigation.

Yet as a Catholic I respond to this news with complicated feelings. It is one thing to toss out the doctrine of Limbo, say, or to drop regulations about abstaining from meat on Friday. The issue raised here is graver.

Rigid Opposition

The consequences of this Catholic mistake have been catastrophic. Cultural prejudice against condoms, often widespread, has been reinforced. Women for whom condoms can be a crucial protection and a method of self-assertion have been kept at risk and disempowered. Priests, nuns, and the few bishops who denounced the condom ban have been disciplined. Catholic lay people who have been savvy enough to ignore it have been put in bad conscience. HIV/AIDS education has been equated with the promotion of promiscuity. Catholic leaders have falsely defined condoms as ineffective. Prevention of illness has been put in opposition to compassion for the sick. Homophobia has been sacralized. The Vatican's rigid adherence to this teaching in the face of monumental human suffering has been central to the broader collapse of Catholic moral authority.

> **FAST FACT**
>
> A 2007 poll sponsored by the group Catholics for Choice found that 90 percent of Catholics in Mexico, 86 percent in Ireland, 79 percent in the United States, 77 percent in the Philippines and 59 percent in Ghana agreed that "using condoms is pro-life because it helps save lives by preventing the spread of AIDS."

HIV/AIDS in Africa, 2005

	Sub-Sarahan Africa	World
New infections	3,200,000	4,900,000
Child (under age 15) infections	630,000	700,000
Deaths	2,400,000	3,100,000
Child deaths	520,000	570,000
People living with HIV/AIDS	25,800,000	40,300,000

Taken from: Africa Renewal from WHO and UNAIDS data.

But even these disasters pale beside the dominant fact of this tragedy: For more than 20 years, the hierarchy's rejection of condom use has been killing people. Even were the Vatican to change its position now—and pray it does—Catholics must still reckon with that betrayal.

Mandatory Vaccinations Against Sexually Transmitted Diseases Are Bad Policy

Kate O'Beirne

The advent of a vaccine against some forms of the human papillomavirus (HPV) occasioned an unusual move. The governor of Texas issued an executive order making this vaccination mandatory for girls entering the sixth grade. In the following article pundit Kate O'Beirne argues that the governor's decision is wrong. Unlike some contagious diseases, HPV cannot spread through casual contact, so there is no reason to suppose that unvaccinated girls would be a threat to others in the sixth grade. Moreover, she notes, the governor is assuming that the vaccine will work well and do no harm. In reality, the Gardasil vaccine is new, and not much is known about its effect on a large population. Those best suited to decide whether the risks are worth the benefits are the parents of girls, she says. Writer O'Beirne is Washington editor for the conservative magazine *National Review*.

O n February 2 [2007], Texas became the first state to require that young girls be vaccinated against some sexually transmitted viruses. This hap-

SOURCE: Kate O'Beirne, "A Mandate in Texas: The Story of a Compulsory Vaccination and What It Means," *National Review*, March 5, 2007, p. 18. Copyright © 2007 National Review Online. Reproduced by permission.

pened when Gov. Rick Perry issued an executive order requiring that students receive a new vaccine before entering the sixth grade. Perry's order has met with criticism from state legislators who object to his unilateral action, medical groups that welcome the breakthrough vaccine but oppose a mandate, and parents who believe that such coercion usurps their authority. The vaccine's manufacturer is aggressively lobbying other state legislatures to back mandates, and legislation to require the new vaccine is pending in over a dozen states.

Last June [2006] the Food and Drug Administration approved Merck & Co.'s Gardasil vaccine for females aged 9 to 26. When administered to girls before they become sexually active, the vaccine can protect against two of the strains of the human papillomavirus (HPV) that cause about 70 percent of cervical cancers. Within a few weeks of the approval, the vaccine was added to the federal list of recommended routine immunizations for eleven- and twelve-year-old girls. The duration of immunity for the three-dose vaccine series, at a cost of about $360, is not yet known. The federal, means-tested Vaccines for Children program will now include the HPV vaccine, and insurance companies are expected to begin covering its costs.

Linked to Cancer

There is little controversy over the recommendation that the vaccine be broadly used. HPV is the most common sexually transmitted infection, with about half of those who are sexually active carrying it at some point in their lives and about 6.2 million infected annually. The number of sexual partners is the most important risk factor for genital HPV infection. There are no treatments to cure HPV infections, but most are cleared by the immune system, with 90 percent disappearing within two years. Some infections do persist, causing genital warts, cancers of the cervix, and other types of cancer. Each year, over 9,000 new cases of cervical cancer are diagnosed, and the

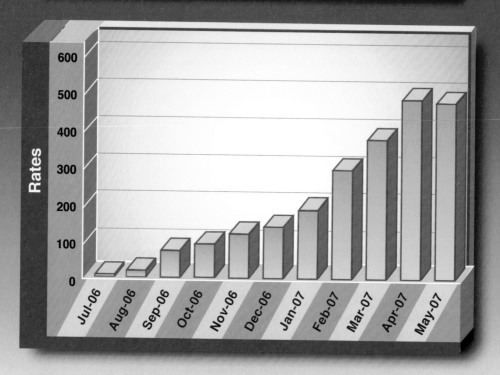

Reports of Adverse Events After Receiving the Gardasil Vaccine Are Increasing

Taken from: National Vaccine Information Center, "Human Papilloma Virus Vaccine Safety: Analysis of Vaccine Adverse Events Reporting System Reports: Part III," August 14, 2007.

disease kills 3,700 women. Routine Pap tests have dramatically reduced the incidence of cervical cancers over the past 50 years, and it is recommended that even those immunized with the new vaccine continue to be tested, as the vaccine doesn't guard against eleven other high-risk strains of HPV that cause cancer.

Governor Perry recognized that "the newly approved HPV vaccine is a great advance in the protection of women's health" in a "whereas" clause on the way to his "therefore" order that rules be adopted to "mandate the age appropriate vaccination of all female children for HPV prior to admission to the sixth grade." In turning a federal recommendation into a state mandate, Perry has thrilled the vaccine manufacturer, while acting against the balance of medical opinion. And critics object to an opt-out provision that puts the onus on parents to file an affidavit seeking approval of their objection.

Opposed by Pediatricians

The American College of Pediatricians opposes requiring the vaccination for school attendance, saying that such a mandate would represent a "serious, precedent-setting action that trespasses on the rights of parents to make medical decisions for their children as well as on the rights of the children to attend school." The chairman of the American Academy of Pediatrics Committee on Infectious Diseases, Dr. Joseph A. Bocchini, believes a vaccine mandate is premature. "I think it's too early," he said. "This is a new vaccine. It would be wise to wait until we have additional information about the safety of the vaccine." The Texas Medical Association also opposes the mandate, expressing concerns over liability and costs.

Mandatory-education laws create a responsibility to make sure that children are vaccinated against contagious diseases they might be exposed to at school. Now states are considering compelling vaccination in the name of a broad public good, even though the disease in question would not be spread at schools.

Dr. Jon Abramson, the chairman of the Advisory Committee on Immunization Practices of the Centers for Disease Control, explains that protecting children against a virus that is spread by sexual activity is different from preventing the spread of measles. Abramson believes that mandating the HPV vaccine "is a much harder case to make, because you're not going to spread it in a school unless you're doing something you're not supposed to be doing in school." Non-vaccinated students would pose no risk to others while at school.

FAST FACT

In addition to protecting against HPV, the Gardasil vaccine is effective against most—but not all—of the viruses that cause genital warts.

Texas state senator Glenn Hegar has introduced legislation to reverse Governor Perry's order on the grounds that research trials are still underway and "such mandates take away parents' rights to make medical decisions for their children and usurp parental authority." Twenty-six of 31 state senators believe the governor has usurped legislative authority too, and are calling on him to rescind the executive order. Perry stands by the order, but the rising controversy has discouraged other supporters of mandates.

Other States Consider Mandates

The *Washington Post* recently reported that Virginia and 17 other states are considering the vaccine requirement "at the urging of New Jersey–based pharmaceutical giant Merck & Co. . . . [which] stands to earn hundreds of millions of

A fourteen-year-old girl receives a shot of human papillomavirus vaccine in response to Texas governor Rick Perry's decree that girls be vaccinated against HPV infection. (Jessica Rinaldi/Reuters/Landov)

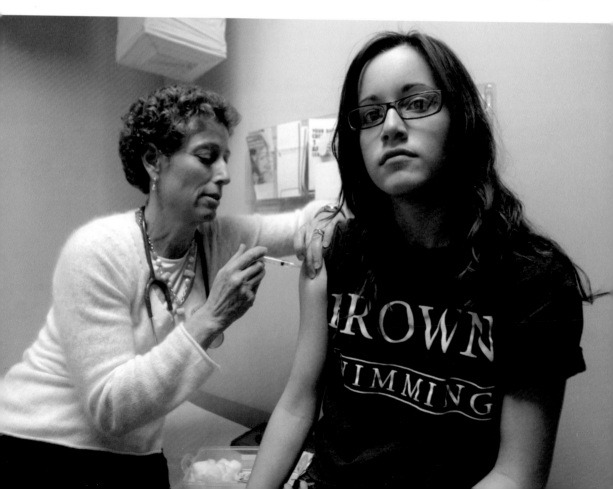

dollars annually on Gardasil, according to Wall Street estimates." Public-health organizations have joined Merck in urging that the vaccine be made available in public clinics and encouraging its coverage by private insurers, but they don't support Merck's push for a school requirement.

There were 210 cases of cervical cancer in Maryland last year. Democratic state senator Delores Kelley introduced a bill to require the HPV vaccine for sixth-grade girls. Following complaints from parents and recent non-compliance problems with current mandated vaccinations, Kelley has withdrawn her bill (though she has spoken openly of reintroducing it next session). She explains that she was unaware of Merck & Co.'s lobbying efforts, and that she learned about the new HPV vaccine through a nonpartisan group of female legislators called Women in Government. More than half of its listed supporters are pharmaceutical manufacturers or other health-related companies. Women in Government is spearheading the campaign to mandate the HPV vaccine through school requirements, and some watchdog groups question the support it receives from Merck & Co. "It's not the vaccine community pushing for this," explains the director of the National Network for Immunization Information. Governor Perry's critics point to his own connection with Gardasil's manufacturer: His former chief of staff is a lobbyist for Merck & Co. in Texas.

The profit motive of a company can coincide with public-health interests, but the case for an HPV-vaccine mandate has not been made. The new vaccine does not prevent cervical cancer, but is a welcome protection against some strains of HPV. It is already available to parents who can decide whether it is appropriate for their young daughters. In substituting his judgment for theirs, Governor Perry has attempted to intrude upon their prerogatives and responsibilities. He has also substituted his own judgment for expert medical opinion. State officials who follow his lead won't enjoy immunity from the firestorm of criticism they will rightly earn.

Mandatory Vaccinations Against Sexually Transmitted Diseases Are Good Policy

Rick Perry

After the Food and Drug Administration approved a new vaccine for human papillomavirus (HPV), the governor of Texas issued an executive order in February 2007 to mandate its use by girls entering the sixth grade. The vaccine, Gardasil, protects against the strains of HPV that are responsible for the majority of cervical cancer cases. However, the Texas legislature swiftly passed a bill countermanding the governor's order. In the following viewpoint Governor Rick Perry defends his order and criticizes the legislature's actions. He emphasizes that his order did not ignore the wishes of parents, since it gave them the right to excuse their daughters from the requirement. He claims that those who oppose his order are insensitive to the suffering of women who needlessly contract cervical cancer. Perry is a Republican who has been governor of Texas since 2000, when he took over the office vacated after George W. Bush became president.

I n early February 2007 I initiated a national debate by ordering the widespread use of the HPV vaccine, which protects women from the deadly human papillomavirus that serves as the most common cause of cervical cancer.

SOURCE: Rick Perry, "Text of Governor Rick Perry's Remarks," in Announcement of Decision Regarding HB 1098, May 8, 2007.

Since then, the legislature has countered that order with the passage of House Bill 1098; a bill which awaits my action by today.

During that timeframe, a debate which affects real lives has been hijacked by politics and posturing.

Widespread Misinformation

I have never seen so much misinformation spread about a vital public health issue: whether it is the effectiveness of the vaccine, the impact of the order on parents' decision-making authority, or the impact this will have on the behavior of young women.

But the fact remains: my order always has been and always will be about protecting women's health.

And while I respect the voice of the legislature, this issue has never been about the separation of powers, but the saving of lives. Those legislators who claim this is about their right to determine public policy have succeeded in overturning my order. But if they care about succeeding in stopping the spread of the second most deadly cancer among women, and not just asserting their power, then they will turn around and pass legislation to make access to the HPV vaccine as widely available as possible.

Instead, they have sent me a bill that will ensure three-quarters of our young women will be susceptible to a virus that not only kills hundreds each year, but causes great discomfort and harm to thousands more. Instead of vaccinating close to 95 percent of our young women, and virtually eliminating the spread of the most common STD in America, they have relegated the lives of our young women to social Darwinism, where only those who can afford it or those who know about the virtues of it will get access to the HPV vaccine.

> **FAST FACT**
>
> The vaccine Gardasil protects against four HPV types that together cause 70 percent of cervical cancers.

Denying Funds for the Poor

In fact, this legislature has not only overturned an order that could save women's lives, but they put rider language in the budget that prevents the state from funding vaccines for low-income women if it is mandated by the commission. This is shameful.

Not only does this not make sense in terms of social policy, it doesn't make fiscal sense. The cost of providing this vaccine to eligible young women through the Vaccines for Children program and Medicaid is less than $13 million in general revenue each year, while the cost of treating HPV-related cervical diseases is $173 million in direct medical costs each year.

I am also mystified by the argument that making this vaccine widely available encourages promiscuity, especially from legislators who voted for a needle exchange program that encourages drug addicts to continue to abuse illegal drugs.

Forgiveness Has Been Forgotten

The fact of the matter is, even when young people are cautious, and abstain from risky behavior, they could still become a victim of HPV, either from a marriage partner, or worse yet, as a victim of rape. Such is the story of Amanda Vail, who was raped and now must forever fight HPV. Amanda, thank you for your courage, and for standing here with me today.

Amanda's story is made all the more tragic by the circumstances surrounding her contracting of this virus. But it is nonetheless a tragedy for every woman who contracts this disease, regardless of the circumstances. And it is the tone of this debate that has disturbed me most. The notion of forgiveness and grace has been totally lost in this debate. People make wrong choices. Our society is full of such individuals who have found redemption from past mistakes.

But if we had a vaccine for lung cancer, would we stop its widespread use because it might send a message that it is okay to engage in an unhealthy behavior like smoking?

The sad irony is, if you or I had a family member suffering from cervical cancer, there is no treatment we would rob them of if it could take away the pain and bring them back to health. And yet, we won't provide them the vaccine that can prevent all that pain and suffering—that death sentence—to begin with because of the message it might send? What about a message of grace, compassion and forgiveness for anyone who has made wrong choices? Have we lost sight of that?

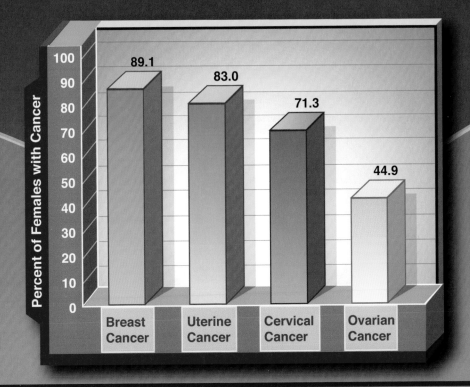

Taken from: U.S. Department of Health and Human Services, *Women's Health USA 2007*.

Texas governor Rick Perry speaks at a news conference on May 8, 2007, about his decree to order young girls to be vaccinated against HPV. (AP Images)

Parents Can Opt Out

Banning widespread access to a vaccine that can prevent cancer is short-sighted policy. Critics cannot legitimately point to science or medicine to back up their claims. Nor can they hide behind the veneer of parental rights when parents can opt out. Nor can they say that it encourages wrong choices with any real legitimacy, and even if they

PERSPECTIVES ON DISEASES AND DISORDERS

could, they do so without regard to a higher imperative: which is to save lives.

And this is not some arcane policy debate. We're talking about real lives. Lives like Barbara Garcia, whose battle with cervical cancer now confines her to a wheelchair. She won't live to see her 9-year-old son one day graduate from high school . . . or ask his sweetheart to marry him. Barbara, thank you for being here today. That's what this is about, my fellow Texans, ensuring that other women don't have to face the same suffering.

It's about women like Cheryl Lieck, the county attorney for Chambers County, who, even though she is a survivor, bears the scars of this terrible disease. After 3 rounds of chemotherapy, 3 intensive surgeries and 37 rounds of radiation, she still must endure pap smears every 3 months. In the end, the fight for her life has cost her more than $250,000. She is fortunate to be alive. Thank you for joining us, Cheryl.

Thousands of women in Texas have stories like Amanda and Barbara and Cheryl. Women who have fought and continue to fight a battle against cervical cancer. In the next year, more than a thousand women will likely be diagnosed with this insidious yet mostly preventable disease. They will begin their fight. I challenge legislators to look these women in the eyes and tell them, "We could have prevented this disease for your daughters and granddaughters, but we just didn't have the gumption to address all the misguided and misleading political rhetoric."

I want to thank those legislators who voted against this bill. They will never have to think twice about whether they did the right thing. No lost lives will occupy the confines of their conscience, sacrificed on the altar of political expediency.

No Veto

I have wrestled for a few days with whether to veto this bill, or let it become law without my signature. But the fact of the matter is, it will become law no matter what because the voice of the Legislature is clear. And rather than allowing this issue to be held captive one more day by legislative politics and the inevitable posturing that will ensue during a veto override debate, I have decided to let it become law without my signature. It is time to move this issue from the political arena to the court of public opinion where real lives are at stake, and it is time to do so without delay.

Every day that goes by, another Texas woman loses her battle with cervical cancer. That is a tragedy. But while those women sadly leave this life, one each day, their voices won't be silenced. Some day they will be heard.

One such voice is that of Heather Burcham, a 31-year old victim from Houston. She was too weak to make the trip here today; cancer is ravaging her body. And when she did come here a few months ago, few in the legislature wanted to listen.

Politicians have had their say on this issue and politics has been served. They have had an opportunity to eliminate the leading cause of the second most common cancer in women. They chose not to.

AIDS Most Likely Originated from Contaminated Vaccines

Brian Martin

When the AIDS epidemic first came to light in the early 1980s, it was a great puzzle to scientists. Within a few years, the majority of scientists agreed that the human immunodeficiency virus (HIV) was responsible. However, the question of how that virus came to infect humans remained open. In the following article social scientist Brian Martin reviews the debate over two leading theories of AIDS origin, both of which assert that HIV began when humans came into contact with a simian immunodeficiency virus (SIV) that affects chimpanzees. The first, known as the bushmeat theory, has the support of a substantial majority of scientists in the field. This theory asserts that humans acquired SIV through direct contact with affected chimpanzees—perhaps through the act of butchering the animals or being bitten by them. However, Martin argues that a second theory, known as the oral polio vaccine (OPV) theory, deserves stronger support. That theory rests on claims that polio vaccines made in the 1950s were contaminated by chimpanzee tissues infected with SIV, which is a precursor to HIV. Martin argues that scientists are prejudiced against this theory, because it would harm their reputations and stir resistance to future vaccination campaigns. Martin is a social scientist at Australia's University of Wollongong; he has written dozens of articles on the OPV theory of AIDS origin.

SOURCE: Brian Martin, "Contested Testimony in Scientific Disputes: The Case of the Origins of AIDS," *The Skeptic*, vol. 13, 2007, p. 52. Copyright © 2007 *The Skeptic*. Reproduced by permission.

For over a decade there has been a fierce debate over how AIDS began that has included disputes over scientific and historical evidence, allegations of dishonesty, defamation suits and a cycle of claims that the challenging theory has been disproved and resurrected. It is widely accepted that most cases of AIDS are due to a simian immunodeficiency virus (SIV) that passed from chimpanzees to humans within the past century, becoming HIV-1 [human immunodeficiency virus] Group M. Disagreement centres around how this transfer occurred.

Two theories have received the bulk of scientific investigation over the past decade. (1) The bushmeat, cut-hunter or natural transfer theory proposes that a hunter, in the course of butchering a chimp, got chimp blood in a cut, or that SIVs were transferred by a chimp biting a human or in the course of some other human-chimp interaction. (2) Oral polio vaccines (OPVs) given to more than a million people in central Africa in the late 1950s were contaminated by chimp SIVs. This is called the polio vaccine or OPV theory.

The origin of AIDS is of more than historical interest. Given that several transfers of SIVs to humans took place about the same time—HIV-2, HIV-1-O and HIV-1-N seem to be independent infections from different SIVs—determining the source of these outbreaks could provide insight in preventing future zoonoses (diseases transmitted from one species to another). If the OPV theory is correct, then searching for surviving individuals who received contaminated vaccine could provide clues about resistance to HIV.

The Theory Fits the Circumstances

The OPV theory focuses on the world's first mass polio vaccination campaign, in central Africa from 1957–1960, using vaccines developed by polio pioneer Hilary Koprowski of the Wistar Institute in Philadelphia. In support of the theory, there is a remarkable coincidence in time and place between the vaccination locations and the earliest known cases of AIDS and HIV+ blood samples, both found predominantly in certain areas in what are today Rwanda, Burundi and the Democratic Republic of the Congo. Polio vaccines were—and in many cases still are—cultured on monkey kidneys, providing a route for SIV contamination. There was no screening of vaccines for SIVs until after their discovery in 1985. There is a precedent: tens of millions of people were given polio vaccines later found to be contaminated by another simian virus, SV40. The theory thus includes a plausible mechanism—contaminated polio vaccines—and fits well with the early epidemiology of AIDS.

Little Support for Bushmeat

The bushmeat theory, in contrast, is poorly developed. It offers no explanation for why SIVs entered humans, and became contagious, in the past century rather than hundreds, thousands or tens of thousands of years ago. It gives no explanation beyond chance for the physical location of the earliest HIV+ and AIDS cases. It can offer no direct evidence of the specific events that led to AIDS. Its advocates typically believe that SIVs entered humans prior to the 1950s but that AIDS maintained a low profile until commerce and urbanization led to wider contacts with infected individuals, though they do not mention the massive flows of humans in Africa prior to the 1950s, for example during the slave trade.

> **FAST FACT**
>
> SV40, a simian virus, was identified in the injected form of polio vaccine in 1960. The next year, the virus was found to cause tumors in rodents, but existing polio vaccine stocks were not recalled and were used until 1963.

The bushmeat theory thus is based on numerous assumptions for which evidence is scant or impossible to obtain. Despite these shortcomings, the bushmeat theory is commonly adopted as the default option: if flaws can be found in the OPV theory, then the bushmeat theory is taken to be true. Thus, the OPV theory is treated by one standard and subject to intense scrutiny and rejected if any apparent flaw is found, while the bushmeat theory is assessed by another standard and subject to little scrutiny and assumed to be true if other theories have any apparent flaws.

The result is a considerable body of literature supporting or opposing the OPV theory, with very little on the bushmeat theory.

Failure to Discredit OPV

More than once, the OPV theory has been pronounced refuted by its opponents. In 1992, a committee set up by the Wistar Institute concluded that the OPV theory was extremely unlikely, using as its definitive evidence the case of a British sailor, David Carr, who apparently died of AIDS in 1959 without having visited Africa: Carr's tissues were found to contain HIV. However, this judgement was premature: a few years later, independent testing of Carr's tissues, with more advanced techniques, found no HIV, and also found cells of another human, suggesting serious deficiencies in the original testing. The mistaken assumption of the OPV critics in this case was that a specific piece of evidence could be definitive.

Some proponents of the bushmeat theory argue that, using HIV's rapid mutation rate, it is possible to work backwards from the diversity of known HIV isolates to calculate a date for a postulated origin point. A prominent "molecular clock" calculation along these lines gave a date of 1931, plus or minus 15 years, well before polio vaccination campaigns, again apparently refuting the OPV theory. Others, though, argue that recombination of HIV variants can give rise to present-day HIV diversity in a much shorter time or that molecular clock calculations are flawed. The lesson from this exchange is that it is unwise to reject a theory solely on the basis of theoretical calculations, because some assumptions underlying the calculations may be flawed.

Democratic Republic of the Congo

The oral polio vaccine (OPV) theory of the origin of the HIV virus focuses on claims of vaccine production and testing in the 1950s in Stanleyville, a city now known as Kisangani, in the African nation now called the Democratic Republic of the Congo.

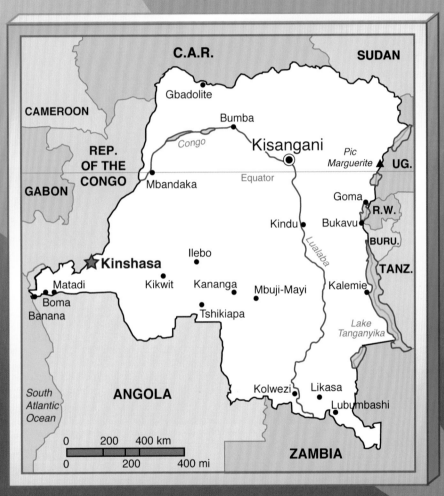

Taken from: University of Texas Library, Index of Maps.

The most likely precursor of HIV-1M is one of the SIVs found in some chimps. The most powerful argument against the OPV theory is that there is no evidence that polio vaccines were ever produced using chimpanzee kidneys. The polio vaccines used in Africa in the

Some scientists believe AIDS can be traced to eating the meat of chimps infected with simian immunodeficiency virus; others argue it was caused by early polio vaccines contaminated by chimp tissues infected with the same virus. (Penny Tweedie/Alamy)

late 1950s—attenuated strains of live polio virus—were developed by the Wistar Institute in Philadelphia and shipped to Africa. Testing of samples provided by the Wistar revealed no SIV, HIV or chimp cells, but instead suggested that the vaccines had been produced using various species of monkeys.

A High-Stakes Clash

The stakes in the origins debate are high. AIDS has killed over 20 million people, with tens of millions more at risk.

If people believed that medical research was responsible, however inadvertently, for the origin of the disease, this would do tremendous damage to the reputation of medicine, and would make many people more apprehensive about vaccinations. This may be the reason why there seems to have been serious resistance to a fair examination of the OPV theory by scientists. Louis Pascal, who first proposed the theory, was unable to find a journal willing to publish any of his articles. After the theory received widespread attention through a 1992 story in *Rolling Stone* by Tom Curtis, polio pioneer Koprowski sued for defamation, causing *Rolling Stone* to drop a subsequent story by Curtis and deterring media coverage of the theory. The settlement of the suit included a "clarification" by *Rolling Stone* that was seized upon by critics of the OPV theory as evidence of scientific capitulation despite it being published under financial duress. The leading journals *Nature* and *Science* have rejected most submissions supportive of the OPV theory; *Science* even rejected a submission by William Hamilton, one of the world's most respected evolutionary biologists. The combination of legal action and the hostility of editors gave the misleading appearance that the theory had been refuted.

[Writer] Edward Hooper's epic book *The River*, first published in 1999, presented extensive new evidence in support of the OPV theory and reopened the origin-of-AIDS debate in both scientific and popular forums. Hooper's UK publisher was subjected to veiled threats of defamation action but did not succumb. The new attention to the OPV theory, plus Hamilton's support, led the Royal Society to hold a discussion meeting on "Origins of HIV and the AIDS epidemic" in September 2000. The agenda for the meeting was manipulated so that a press conference, held on the first day of the two-day event, was just after the announcement of the tests on Wistar vaccines that gave the superficial appearance that the

OPV theory had been refuted. In this and other ways, the Royal Society meeting became a means for scientists antagonistic to the OPV theory to attempt to demolish it in a way that could be deemed authoritative and definitive.

New Life for OPV?

At the Royal Society meeting, Hooper announced new evidence suggesting that polio vaccines used in the 1957–1960 vaccination campaigns might have been prepared in Africa. This meant that the tests of Wistar vaccine were far from fatal for the OPV theory. However, due to the way the meeting was organised, Hooper's new claims received little publicity. Following the meeting, Hooper found new evidence that batches of polio vaccine were prepared in African laboratories in order to boost their titre and enable vaccination of more people. Hooper interviewed Africans who in the late 1950s worked at the Laboratoire Médical de Stanleyville (LMS) and the nearby research camp at Lindi, where more than 500 chimps were sacrificed from 1956–1959. The evidence from these workers suggested that chimp kidneys may have been used at the LMS to prepare polio vaccines. Growing new vaccine batches locally would have reduced the amounts needed to be shipped from the U.S. or Belgium. Hooper has . . . obtained support for this scenario in interviews conducted with Americans and Europeans who had direct dealings with LMS and Lindi in the 1950s. . . .

Testimonial evidence, though central to the current debate on the origin of AIDS, has to be treated as only one component in a wider picture including phylogenetic [concerning evolutionary development], epidemiological [the study of disease in a population] and archival evidence. Although testimony currently seems to favour the OPV theory, new contrary testimonial evidence could come to light, or other sorts of new evidence might be treated as definitive. A similar set of considerations applies to the bushmeat theory.

AIDS Most Likely Did Not Originate from Contaminated Vaccines

Paul Osterrieth

In 1999 author Edward Hooper published a book called *The River* in which he argued that AIDS originated in an oral polio vaccine (OPV) contaminated with chimpanzee cells infected by a simian virus; the virus later mutated to cause AIDS. Since then the so-called OPV theory of AIDS origin has been knocked down several times, only to be revived by its supporters. The latest version of the OPV theory rests on claims that the contamination took place in the late 1950s during the production of polio vaccine in Stanleyville (now Kisangani), a city in the northeast region of the Democratic Republic of the Congo. In the following viewpoint Paul Osterrieth, the researcher at the center of the accusations, rebuts the charges. Although he was working in the Stanleyville lab at the time, he says he never produced polio vaccine. Moreover, he argues, others there lacked the technical know-how, facilities, or motivation to do so. He describes the claims that AIDS could have originated in the Stanleyville lab as fantasy. Osterrieth, who died in 2007, was a microbiologist who went on to become a professor in the Pathology Department at the University of Liege in Belgium.

SOURCE: Paul Osterrieth, "Oral Polio Vaccine: Fact Versus Fiction," *Vaccine*, January 2004, p. 1,831. Copyright © 2004 Elsevier Ltd. All rights reserved. Reproduced with permission from Elsevier.

It is well known that infections can occur after medical interventions because of a lack of sterility; to imagine that such could be the case with vaccinations may therefore appear to be a conceivable hypothesis which then must be verified on basis of facts. As many vaccines are produced in living cells, any adventitious [unwanted] infectious agent present in those cells may represent a potential danger. Well aware of this risk, vaccine manufacturers test their products with all available tests, but evidently they cannot check against the presence of the unknown. This is what Mr. Edward Hooper [proponent of the OPV theory] says, but he goes one step further by affirming that a contaminating agent *was* present and that an accident *did* occur. After having suggested several prior hypotheses and having to eliminate these on basis of factual evidence, Hooper now says that HIV was introduced into humans in Kisangani, Democratic Republic of the Congo (formerly Stanleyville, Belgian Congo) because oral polio vaccine (OPV) was produced there in SIV-infected chimpanzee kidney cells.

As Mr. Hooper, acting like a prosecutor, goes on and on with his theory about this alleged origin of HIV, and as I, his designated defendant, am the target of his wild accusations, I feel obliged to provide precise additional information on what actually happened in the Laboratoire Médical de Stanleyville (LMS) during the 1950s, beyond any already given.

A Ramshackle Lab

When I arrived in 1956, the LMS was located in a very old building that was extended on several sides by small additions covered by prolongations of a corrugated iron roof. It was a miserable place, extremely hot and overcrowded with men and material. For example, the cleaning and sterilization of glassware and culture media were carried out under a simple roof with no walls. It was miraculous that one could manage to perform bacterial cultures and analysis in such surroundings. . . .

Hooper reports that [lab director] Dr. [Ghislain] Courtois had the knowledge to carry out tissue culture on the basis of notes he took at the Oswaldo Cruz Institute, and that he did produce tissue culture in the old LMS as early as 1956. That Dr. Courtois made tissue culture in the old LMS must be discarded as fantasy for many reasons: the lab was an awfully overcrowded place, hot and dirty, where it would be hard to try to carry out tissue culture. Moreover, to my knowledge, Dr. Courtois had no practical experience at all in tissue culture; he mainly administered the lab, took care of relations with other services, examined liver slides for evidence of yellow fever, and inoculated mice with the help of Madame Paula Liègois and Mr. Victor Amunga. That he carried out tissue culture from chimpanzees is pure fantasy: extending this fantasy to Dr. [Gaston] Ninane's laboratory is [within LMS] delirium. . . .

Did Needles Give Rise to HIV?

Some researchers, while rejecting the oral polio vaccine (OPV) theory of the origin of HIV, believe that the repeated use of unsterilized needles transferred simian immunodeficiency virus (SIV) from person to person in Africa until the virus evolved into HIV.

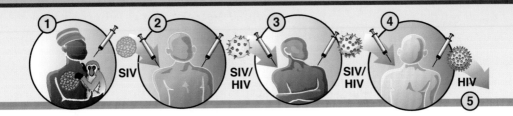

Taken from: William Carlsen, "Did Modern Medicine Spread an Epidemic?" *San Francisco Chronicle*, January 15, 2001.

Chimp Camp

When I joined the laboratory in 1956, the Lindi Camp for chimpanzees was already established in the forest on the far side of the Lindi River. I do not know exactly when it was opened. However, whereas it was not a secret place, it was restricted to visitors as a precaution against spread of infectious agents. Because of these precautions, few people knew exactly what was going on there, and many rumors could circulate owing to ignorance among lay people of microbiology [the study of microorganisms like bacteria and viruses] and epidemiology [the study of disease in a population] laboratories. One could afford no risk of chimpanzees infecting humans or of humans infecting chimpanzees. . . .

The chimpanzees were housed in cages built of wooden planks and wire mesh. Each harbored two chimpanzees, but the animals were separated by a wooden wall and there were separate entrances so that each chimp was in fact alone, which was necessary for handling, although very young ones were kept together. Bonobos [a variety of chimps smaller than the common chimp] were sometimes in one side of a divided unit with a common chimp occupying the other side.

Lindi Camp was established to test polio vaccines, but as the chimpanzees were available, other experiments were carried out to obtain a full return on investment. Chimpanzees were not killed for tissue culture purposes, but to check the results of experiments involving poliomyelitis, hepatitis, and other pathogens [disease-causing organisms]. Many chimpanzees died of illnesses or malnutrition, but I have no exact data regarding specific causes of death. It is inconceivable that serum or tissues from dead animals or from animals sacrificed after experiments could be used for tissue culture purposes.

FAST FACT

In 2004 a team of researchers showed that the simian immunodeficiency virus (SIV) infecting chimpanzees is genetically unrelated to HIV-1, the virus thought to have started the AIDS epidemic. For most scientists, this is conclusive proof that the oral polio vaccine (OPV) theory is wrong, but its proponents dispute the claims.

Mr. Hooper has greatly exaggerated my role at Lindi Camp. If [lab workers] Antoine and Joseph say I was the one who did most of the autopsies, they are wrong; that was the job of Dr. Ninane. I might have helped from time to time, when necessary, but not more. I did not perform autopsies even if I happened to be present by chance when Dr. Ninane was performing one. However, based on my observations of those autopsies that I did attend, organs were removed with aseptic precautions as they should be, particularly if they had to be checked for bacterial infection or sent to Dr. F. Deinhardt at Philadelphia Children's Hospital for work on his hepatitis project. Blood was also taken for serology, but in limited quantity (laymen frequently overestimate the quantity of blood taken). Postmortem blood or tissues are not useful, as bacteria from the gut quickly disseminate and sterility is no longer possible. Because of tropical conditions, it was good practice to store all biological samples in the cold. . . .

Bacterial Studies

My initial duties in Stanleyville were bacteriological. I published with Pierre Doupagne a paper on the incidence of different bacteria in cultures of human urine. . . . To argue, as Mr. Hooper does, that my real task was to prepare vaccine, is to fly in the face of all documented facts.

Although the documentary evidence is all negative, I want to respond specifically to Hooper's allegations regarding chimpanzee cell culture. I repeat that the laboratory was not an ideal location for cell culture. We had one freezer, which often failed, a centrifuge for serum separation, and our hood was simply a box with a UV light. . . .

Had we been able to make polio vaccine, one can imagine how we would have been proud and boasted about it in the annual report!

Chimpanzee kidneys were not used because they originated from diseased or experimental animals, because they were from a relatively expensive and rare species,

The author of the article insists that he did not sacrifice chimpanzees to obtain blood for tissue cell culture while working at the Stanleyville laboratory. (Todd Muskopf/Alamy)

because from our work we knew that chimpanzees could acquire human infections, and because they were not a well-characterized substrate for virus isolation (or for that matter, vaccine production).

The idea that we might have used chimpanzee sera for cell culture is also false. . . .

No Vaccine Tampering

While I was at Stanleyville the source of CHAT virus [a type of polio vaccine] and other attenuated OPV strains was from the Wistar Institute [where the vaccine was destroyed] sent as frozen concentrated stock. The transport from Philadelphia to Stanleyville could be achieved quickly under refrigerated conditions. . . .

Hooper insists that the vaccine was "amplified" locally in Stanleyville. I have already explained why this was not feasible, but in addition there was no need to do so. However, dilution of the concentrated stock was necessary before administration, and I probably did do some of that work. . . .

My virus unit in the new LMS had two rooms, one of which contained a centrifuge, while the other was a sterile room for attempts at cell culture. The cell culture room was flooded day and night with UV light and locked. I was the only person to enter, as I needed to master the techniques under primitive conditions, far different from those at CDC [Centers for Disease Control and Prevention, in Atlanta, Georgia]! Apparently some local people remember that I stayed alone in the evenings in the sterile room. This was not for reason of secrecy, but merely not to be disturbed during my attempts at cell culture work. Once more, I solemnly state that I never produced polio vaccine of any sort, never attempted to multiply polio virus, and never attempted to culture chimpanzee cells.

Faulty Testimony

When one examines carefully Mr. Hooper's presentation it becomes clear that the only "evidence" for his hypothesis is the memories of some elderly people who had indirect and partial knowledge of the work circumstances some 48 years ago. . . .

I must . . . give some information about the Congolese technicians in the era of Belgian administration. The Congolese who came to work with us only received limited training as nurses or nurses' aides, with little scientific background. In the late 1950s, the administration's aim was to school progressively the native population. For example, a school for training medical assistants (Ecole pour Assistants Médicaux Indigènes) was founded at that time. Several large laboratories opened in the late fifties, like the new LMS in 1957, in anticipation of independence. These were built with Belgian Congo funds. Sadly, subsequent to independence, internal ethnic divisions, terrorism and disorganization resulted largely in destruction of the scientific infrastructure. . . .

I want to reiterate that I did not participate in any program of sacrificing chimpanzees in order to obtain organs and/or blood for tissue culture purpose. I did not prepare CHAT or other OPV in cell culture. In particular, I never prepared chimpanzee cell culture. . . .

Moreover, I have never purposely given misleading answers to anyone about my work in Stanleyville. Mr. Hooper constantly implies that "secrets" have been maintained for over 40 years, and relies on testimony of people with limited education or scientific background and only with second or third hand knowledge, despite documented evidence to the contrary. Scientists are notoriously poor at keeping secrets, and it does not fit at all with scientific culture.

Mr. Hooper's method is to take any word slip or hesitation and to convert it into a mysterious allusion to hidden crimes. This is the way of a prosecutor, not an investigator, and it has more to do with science fiction than fact.

Abstinence Education Is the Best Way to Prevent the Spread of STDs

Daniel Allott

The widespread phenomenon of teen pregnancy has raised concerns about the spread of sexually transmitted diseases as well as the birth of babies to unmarried teens. In the following viewpoint analyst Daniel Allott examines the two main approaches to discouraging teen pregnancy, known as "safe sex" and "abstinence only." The former, he says, supposedly deters teens from premarital sex but in reality focuses principally on the use of contraceptives, especially condoms. A major problem with this approach, he says, is that contraceptives are imperfect. Even barriers like condoms cannot prevent the spread of all STDs. By contrast, abstinence—that is, refraining from engaging in sex prior to marriage—is guaranteed to prevent STD infection. Moreover, Allott argues, abstinence education works, in part because teens fear contracting STDs. Indeed, he claims that abstinence education is responsible for much of the observed decline in teen pregnancy. Allott is a policy analyst for American Values, a conservative nonprofit organization dedicated to protecting life and preserving marriage and the family.

SOURCE: Daniel Allott, "Educating Responsibility: Is Abstinence Education Best for Our Children?" American Values, September 1, 2004. Reproduced by permission.

Debates concerning sex education have concentrated on two distinct approaches: "safe sex" courses allegedly teach at least some abstinence for teens but in fact primarily focus on teaching teens to use contraceptives, especially condoms, when having sex. A second approach, called abstinence education, promotes and encourages teens to delay sexual activity, usually until marriage.

High Rates of Teen Pregnancy

The United States has witnessed a 20 percent decline in its teenage pregnancy rate since 1991. Declines have occurred among all age groups, races, and in all states. There are many factors that have contributed to this decline including increased education about sexually transmitted diseases, changes in welfare policy that, among other things, cracked down on fathers for child support, as well as increased availability of contraceptives and a move towards more conservative, religiously-based attitudes on sex. At the same time, policymakers, politicians, and the general public agree that more needs to be done. American adolescents still have pregnancy, birth and abortion rates twice as high as those in Canada and Great Britain, and three times as high as France and Sweden. Each year one million teenage women, ten percent of all women aged 15–19, become pregnant. . . .

Adolescent pregnancy and STDs [sexually transmitted diseases] carry significant social costs. These costs are borne out by the teenagers themselves, by society, and by the children of teen mothers. Beyond the social costs are the financial ones which are measured in billions of dollars. Indeed, for the individuals involved, and for society as a whole, unmarried adolescent motherhood is something to be deterred. The statistics reveal, however, that teen mothers are not a random sample of the population. Teens that give birth are much more likely to be non-white, come from poor or low-income families, and one-half of pregnant teens receive inadequate pre-natal care. So, while teenage pregnancy trends may be headed in the right direction, much more needs to be accomplished. . . .

Two Approaches

The individuals and groups attempting to reduce teen pre-marital sexual activity and births fall roughly into two groups. The first holds that programs must give teens a single, unambiguous message that sex outside of marriage is wrong and harmful to their physical and mental health, while the second tells teens they should not have sex, but if they do, they should practice so called "safe sex," which involves using contraceptives. In view of the fact that the Bush administration has recently [2004] proposed doubling spending on abstinence programs, a thoughtful examination on the merits of each approach is needed.

The Use of Contraception

There has been an increase in the percentage of adolescent females who report using any contraceptive method at first sex. In 1982, less than half of females ages 15–19 used a contraceptive during first sex. By 1995, three-fourths of girls in this age group reported using some form of contraceptive at first sex. In addition:

- Of the 2.7 million teenage women who use contraceptives, 44 percent use the contraceptive pill.
- About 1 in 6 teenage women practicing contraception combine two methods, primarily the male condom and another method.

Over the past 30 years, states have expanded minors' ability to consent to contraceptives, which reflects the US Supreme Court's ruling extending the constitutional right to privacy to a minor's right to obtain contraceptives. At the moment, 20 states and the District of Columbia explicitly allow all minors to consent to contraceptive services and 14 others allow minors to consent to contraceptive services in one or more circumstances. Groups like the Sex Information and Education Council of the US (SIECUS) and Advocates for Youth receive over $400 million annually from the US government to fund sex education and contraception education. Although these groups allegedly promote a curriculum that takes a middle position—providing a strong abstinence message while also talking about contraception—in reality most of these programs contain little or no meaningful abstinence material. Consequently, the proportion of teenagers having sex has increased in the past two decades. Social norms that once condemned sex outside of marriage have become far more permissive. A 1997 Child Trends study reported that boys in particular are teased or taunted if they are not sexually active while those who have multiple partners often gain in reputation. Often, girls will have sex to maintain relationships. These pressures from peers are reinforced by the popular media that glamorizes sex, and by adults who are ambivalent about their own values or insufficiently involved in their teenagers' lives.

FAST FACT

For 2007 the administration of President George W. Bush expanded the focus of its abstinence-only initiative to include unmarried people up to the age of twenty-nine.

Shortcomings of Sex Ed

Sex education has been no panacea. Sex and contraceptive education is now available in over 90 percent of high schools and most teens are fully informed about how pregnancies occur. One problem is that no matter how well used, no contraceptive is perfect. In fact, with perfect use, the condom—the most commonly used contraceptive among teenagers—has a failure rate of three percent. Typical use failure rates are 15 percent for condoms, 30 percent for spermacides, and eight percent for the contraceptive pill.

Studies that examine the effects of teenage reports on sex education in schools are quite dubious. Some studies show that sex education is linked to decreased sexual activity, while others conclude that teens' participation in sex education classes is associated with a higher risk of pregnancy and childbirth. In addition, providing contraceptives to students via school-based health clinics is not always associated with earlier or increased sexual activity in teens but this practice has not been found to reduce pregnancy or birthrates for adolescents either. Surveys indicate that knowledge about contraceptives may give youth a false sense of security, not only from pregnancy but STDs.

In addition, contraceptives fail to take into account the possible emotional effects of teenage sexual activity. Teens who engage in pre-marital sex are likely to experience fear about pregnancy and STDs, guilt, regret, lowered self-respect, fear of commitment, and depression. Pre-marital sex can also cause teens to marry less favorably. A study of college freshman found that non-virgins with multiple sex partners were more likely to view marriage as difficult and involving a loss of personal freedom and happiness. Virgins were more likely to view marriage as enjoyable. Also, a 2003 Heritage Foundation study found that sexually active teenagers are more likely to be depressed and to attempt suicide, all else held equal.

In fact, girls who were sexually active were three times as likely to attempt suicide (14 percent) than girls who were not sexually active in this study.

Parents Support Abstinence Programs

Abstinence programs strongly encourage abstaining from sexual activity during the teen years, and preferably until marriage. They teach that casual sex at an early age not only poses serious threats of pregnancy and infection by STDs, but also can undermine an individual's capacity to build loving, intimate relationships as an adult, and interfere with their life goals, education, and career building. These programs encourage teen abstinence as a preparation and pathway to healthy adult marriage. . . .

There is little doubt that public opinion has progressed such that more parents and teens prefer abstinence education to traditional sex education. "Kids are saturated with information about contraception and messages about encouraging casual, permissive sex" said Robert Rector, who helped write the Bush administration's abstinence education program. In fact, teens want to be taught abstinence. A 2000 poll found that 93 percent of teenagers believe that teens should be given a strong message from society to abstain from sex until at least after high school. Parents, too, want their children to be taught that sex should be linked to marriage. Data drawn from a Zogby International poll of parents in December 2003 found that very few parents support basic themes of comprehensive sex-ed courses. In fact, 80 percent of parents want young people taught that sex should at least be delayed until after high school. And only seven percent want teens to be taught that sexual activity in high school is okay. Also, only eight percent of parents believed that teaching about contraceptives is more important than teaching about abstinence.

Abstinence Education Is Effective

According to the Physicians Resource Council, the drop in teen birth rates during the 1990's was due primarily to increased sexual abstinence. From 1988 to 1995, sexual activity among unwed boys aged 15 to 19 dropped from 60 to 55 percent. There are over 1000 abstinence until marriage programs in the United States. Most started by non-profit or faith-based organizations, these programs teach young people the skills needed to practice abstinence, including self-esteem building, self-control, decision-making, goal setting, character education and communication skills, and the reality of parenthood.

Despite opponents' assertions, abstinence programs have been proven to work. Choosing the Best, an abstinence program based in Georgia and started in 1993, developed a curriculum and materials that are used in over two thousand school districts in 48 states. The results have been quite notable. For example, Choosing the Best's materials were used in all 8th grade classes for a period of four years in certain school districts in Georgia. A study by the Georgia State Board of Education examined the effectiveness of this curriculum and found a 38 percent reduction in sexual activity among middle school students, while districts that didn't use abstinence-based

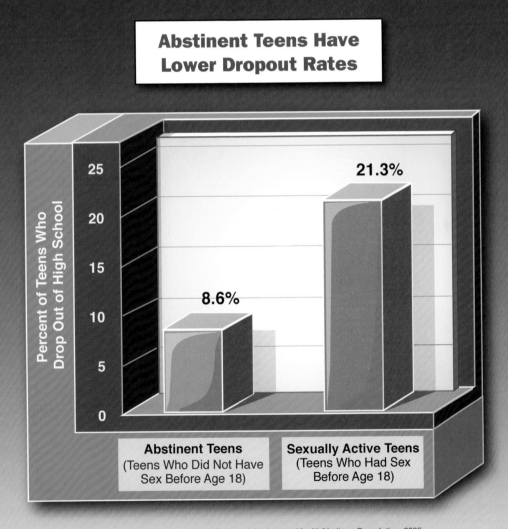

Abstinent Teens Have Lower Dropout Rates

Percent of Teens Who Drop Out of High School

21.3%

8.6%

| Abstinent Teens (Teens Who Did Not Have Sex Before Age 18) | Sexually Active Teens (Teens Who Had Sex Before Age 18) |

Taken from: National Longitudinal Survey of Adolescent Health/Heritage Foundation, 2005.

education experienced an average of a six percent reduction during the same years.

STDs Deter Some Teens

Another reason why teens are abstaining from sex at a higher rate is the increased prevalence of sexually transmitted disease among youths.

An instructor teaches an abstinence class at an Alabama middle school. Students there are strongly discouraged from sexual activity until marriage. (Jerry Ayres/ Newhouse News Service/ Landov)

- Every year 3 million teens—about one in 4 sexually experienced teens—acquires an STD.
- Chlamydia is more common among teens than among older men and women. In some settings 10 to 30 percent of sexually active women and 10 percent of teenage men tested for STDs have been found to have Chlamydia.
- Teens have higher rates of gonorrhea than do sexually active men and women aged 20–44.

If these common diseases are not treated they can lead to a variety of ailments including: pelvic inflammatory disease, infertility, and ectopic pregnancy. Studies have found that up to 15 percent of sexually active teenage women are infected with the human papilloma virus (HPV), an incurable virus that is present in nearly all cervical cancers. No contraceptive offers 100 percent protection against STDs. In fact, the Bush administration has just announced [2004] it is considering requiring warning labels on condom packages noting that they do not protect users from all STDs. Most recent studies indicate that condoms do not safeguard against HPV and other viruses. By promoting traditional sex and contraception-based education in schools, we are not only exposing our children to the risk of pregnancy and emotional problems, but to the devastating and life-changing effects of sexually transmitted diseases.

Abstinence Brings Positive Results

Although some research has found that the use of contraceptives was the main reason for declines in pregnancy and birth rates over the past 15 years—accounting for between 50 and 80 percent of the difference—a new study published in the *Adolescent and Family Health Journal* found that among unmarried teenage girls ages 15 to 19, increased abstinence accounted for nearly 70 percent of the reduction in pregnancy rate between 1991 and 1995.

In the end, sex education programs that teach teenagers about their bodies, but not how to deal with their feelings for one another and the values that should guide their relationships, fail. At the same time, "just say no" campaigns will not do much better if they fail to engage young people in constructive activities and offer alternatives to the pro-sex messages they are receiving from virtually every other influence in their lives. Experimental studies indicate that adolescents involved in community volunteer service programs and programs that focus on youth development, including involvement in such activities as educational mentoring, employment, sports, or the performing arts, have a strong impact on adolescent sexual activity. For the past two decades, contraceptives have been widely available to teens, and while pregnancy rates have declined, they are still much too high, and STDs are a problem that is beyond the scope of any contraceptive method. Abstinence until marriage education is the only way to ensure our children can lead healthy, responsible lives.

Abstinence Education Is Not the Best Way to Prevent the Spread of STDs

Amanda Schaffer

Abstinence-only sex education programs have been increasingly favored by elected officials. Questions remain, however, about their effectiveness. In the following viewpoint writer Amanda Schaffer argues that abstinence-only programs are a waste of money and should be ended. She cites a study by Mathematica Policy Research, which she says was conducted with scientific rigor. It followed a cohort of two thousand students over a period of seven years. Those randomly assigned to abstinence-only programs showed no more inclination to abstain from sex during their teen years than those who did not participate in the abstinence programs. That means a billion dollars in federal funding has been wasted, she says. Worse yet, Schaffer argues, abstinence education programs tend to spread misinformation. However, the research has not deterred the Bush administration from seeking more funding for abstinence programs, she adds. Schaffer is a science and medicine columnist for the online magazine *Slate*.

SOURCE: Amanda Schaffer, "No More Virginal: Spend $1 Billion on Abstinence. Get Nothing." *Slate,* April 20, 2007. Copyright 2007 *Washington Post.* Newsweek Interactive Co., LLC. All rights reserved. Distributed by United Feature Syndicate, Inc.

In the past decade, the federal government has spent more than $1 billion on programs that promote abstinence as the only healthy choice to make about sex before marriage. Last week [April 2007], the government's own long-term evaluation of the initiatives, required by Congress in 1997, showed that these programs seem to accomplish essentially nothing. That's right: Nada. Students in the programs were no more likely to abstain from sex than their peers. And if they did lose their virginity, they tended to do so at the same average age and have the same number of sexual partners as other students did. As Rep. Henry Waxman, D-Calif., put it, "In short, Ameri-

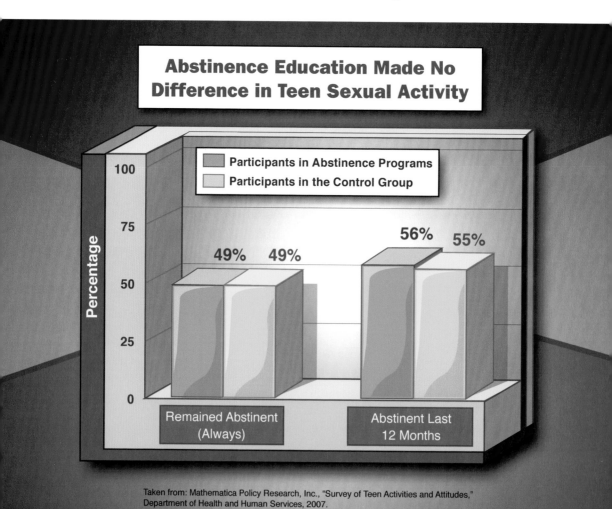

Abstinence Education Made No Difference in Teen Sexual Activity

Taken from: Mathematica Policy Research, Inc., "Survey of Teen Activities and Attitudes," Department of Health and Human Services, 2007.

can taxpayers appear to have paid over 1 billion federal dollars for programs that have no impact."

The new study, rigorously conducted by Mathematica Policy Research Inc. on behalf of the government, should be the death knell for abstinence-only programs, which have also drawn criticism for perpetuating gender stereotypes, spreading medical inaccuracies, and ignoring the separation of church and state. While the Bush administration shows few signs of rethinking this pet project, a growing number of states have begun to wise up, rejecting millions in federal funding because they come with abstinence strings attached. The problem is that even larger sums of federal money now bypass state governments and flow directly to community abstinence groups, often in the form of multiyear grants, with little or no oversight. It's up to Congress to stanch this ooze.

No Effects Found

The Mathematica study is long-term and has scientific bona fides that are hard to dispute. The researchers focused on four abstinence-only education programs—in Virginia, Florida, Wisconsin, and Mississippi—that received federal money through a program called Title V. Beginning in 1999, the researchers randomly assigned more than 2,000 students either to receive or not to receive abstinence-only instruction, in addition to whatever else they did in school. Then in 2005–06, when the students were on average 16½, the researchers surveyed both groups about their sexual attitudes, knowledge, and behavior. Remarkably, those who'd gotten the abstinence-only ed—some as often as every school day for up to four years—did not behave differently than their peers.

The abstinence-taught teens were no more likely to abstain from sex or even to wait longer before losing their virginity. (In both groups, those who'd had sex did so for the first time at an average age just shy of 15.) The abstinence-taught kids knew as much as the others about the risks of unprotected sex and the consequences of sexually transmitted diseases and were just as likely to use a condom. That's the good news—though it's contradicted by previous work by sociologists Peter Bearman and Hannah Brückner that suggested kids who pledge to be abstinent until marriage are less likely to protect themselves with condoms if and when they do have sex.

States May Balk

Undeterred by the Mathematica findings—"new and diverse abstinence programs have grown around the country" since the research began in the 1990s, the Department of Health and Human Services said in a statement—President Bush has asked for $191 million for abstinence education for fiscal year 2008, an increase of $28 million over this fiscal year.

But the states may refuse to take the money that flows through them. States are required to match 75 percent of the funds they receive for abstinence ed through Title V, and this can jeopardize other priorities. Also, teaching abstinence must be the "exclusive purpose" of programs paid for out of this federal pot. Programs cannot promote the use of condoms or contraception, and they must tell kids that sex outside of marriage is "likely to have harmful psychological and physical effects." Given that the public is largely unconvinced by this rigid approach—and that government reports reveal medical inaccuracies in abstinence curricula, not to mention this month's evidence that abstinence-ed doesn't make kids more abstinent—it's no wonder that more and more governors are choosing to bail.

Ohio Gov. Ted Strickland announced recently that his state would withdraw from Title V for the coming year, rejecting more than $1 million in federal funds and also freeing about $500,000 in the state budget. (As a spokesman explained, "[I]f the state is going to spend money on teaching and protecting kids, the governor believes it is better to spend it in a smarter, more comprehensive approach.") New Jersey, Wisconsin, Connecticut, Rhode Island, Montana, and Maine have also pulled out or plan to do so by the end of the year. (And California never participated to begin with.) The Sexuality Information and Education Council of the United States, a policy and advocacy group, estimates that together, these eight states are turning down about $11 million of the total $50 million allocated to the Title V program.

Dollars Flow to Morality Groups

But the rest of that $50 million is only part of the problem. In 2000, another federal cookie jar opened. Community-Based Abstinence Education, as the initiative is now called, channels money directly to community groups rather than through state governments. And starting last year, the grant processes and rules were changed. Now partici-pants have to focus *less* on measurable public health goals

Ohio governor Ted Strickland announced in 2007 that his state would withdraw from Title V, rejecting federal funds for abstinence programs. Many state governors have also opted out of the program. **(AP Images)**

and *more* on chastity as a form of moral virtue. Programs "must not . . . refer to abstinence as a form of contraception," but should teach that "abstinence reflects qualities of personal integrity and is honorable," according to the new guidelines. (Programs should also teach students to watch out for corrupt classmates, avoiding "parties where sexually active peers are likely to attend.") The length of grants was increased to five years, which means fewer opportunities for oversight. And so far, Congress hasn't helped either. Congressional earmarks to abstinence-only groups, like the Abstinence Clearinghouse and the Medical Institute, continue apace.

Now that the Democrats are in control, they need to crack down. The current funding for Title V expires in June [2007] and, given this latest study, should expire for good. As for money that flows directly to community groups, Congress could cut this, too, despite the five-year grants, to decrease the number of new grants offered or possibly reduce payments to existing grantees. Now that the government has collected its own evidence that teaching about abstinence doesn't make kids less sexually active, it's time to redirect money to comprehensive sex ed. The kind that teaches kids to protect themselves with condoms and is much more likely to do some good.

FAST FACT

For teens taking part in a scientific study by Mathematica Policy Research, the average age at which they first had sex was identical for those in the abstinence and the control groups: 14.9 years.

Pregnant Women Should Be Tested for Herpes

Zane A. Brown and Carolyn Gardella

Herpes is an infectious disease that can have worrisome implications, especially for prospective mothers. In the following article Zane A. Brown, a physician and professor who has advocated widely for universal herpes testing for pregnant mothers, and Carolyn Gardella, his colleague at the University of Washington, discuss advances in testing and why they should be routinely employed for pregnant women. They note that most of the estimated 45 million infected Americans are unaware of their status. A million more Americans, mostly young, acquire the infection each year. Therefore, the authors state, new strategies to increase testing are needed. Among their recommendations are that pregnant women undergo blood tests for the herpes virus in order to avoid putting their babies at risk during the final stages of pregnancy. Brown is a professor in the University of Washington's Department of Obstetrics and Gynecology. He serves as a paid speaker for GlaxoSmithKline, which manufactures herpes-control medications. Gardella is an assistant professor in the Division of Women's Health at the University of Washington. In addition to being a physician, she holds a master's degree in public health.

SOURCE: Zane A. Brown and Carolyn Gardella, "Serologic Testing for Herpes Simplex Virus: Ready for Prime Time?" *Contemporary OB/GYN*, October 1, 2007. All rights reserved. Reproduced by permission.

Underdiagnosis and lack of symptoms are fueling the genital herpes crisis in the United States. Of the 1.6 million new cases of genital herpes in this country each year, most are transmitted by persons who are unaware that they're even infected—because their infections are subclinical or undiagnosed. But accurate serologic tests [studying antibodies in blood serum] to detect HSV [herpes simplex virus] antibodies and distinguish between HSV-1 and HSV-2 infection exist and in our opinion should be used routinely to diagnose herpes infections in symptomatic persons and in asymptomatic persons at risk for having or acquiring the infection.

How Huge Is the Epidemic?

At least 45 million people older than age 12 are infected with genital herpes, by current estimates. Put another way, one out of five adolescents and adults are infected, with the prevalence higher in women than men. Recent NHANES [National Health and Nutrition Examination Survey] data suggest a drop in the prevalence of HSV-2 for the first time since the survey began in the 1980s. However, with more than 1 million Americans acquiring genital HSV-2 every year, the epidemic is expected to continue in the near future. Furthermore, there's been a concomitant increase in genital herpes caused by HSV-1. Among college students with newly diagnosed genital herpes, 80% were from HSV-1. The rise in genital HSV-1 is likely due to increased practice of orogenital [oral] sex, perceived by people in this age group as a safe alternative to genital-genital sex.

Although one in five persons has genital herpes, it bears repeating that most people with it don't know they carry the virus. Lack of diagnosis of the infection is therefore a key contributor to the epidemic. Seventy percent of genital herpes infections are transmitted by people who either have no symptoms or are unaware of their infections.

Herpes Infections Are Most Common During Childbearing Years

Percent of Total Respondents

60
50
40
30
20
10
0

0–11 12–17 18–24 25–44 45–64 65+ No answer

Age Range

Taken from: Herpes.org, "Herpes.org survey, 2002–2006."

More and Better Testing Is Needed

Strategies to increase testing and diagnosis of genital herpes infections are important. The Centers for Disease Control and Prevention [CDC] recommends laboratory confirmation of genital herpes because the clinical diagnosis is neither sensitive nor specific. Up to 20% of patients with symptoms are incorrectly diagnosed as having HSV when they do not.

For women who present with a genital lesion, a specimen for viral culture can be collected and viral typing performed. The main disadvantages of viral culture are difficulty in handling and the high false-negative rate. Up to 75% of viral cultures from recurrent lesions are negative.

Alternatively, polymerase chain reaction (PCR) detects HSV DNA in lesions or from genital secretions. Not only is it three to four times more sensitive than viral culture, but the specimen requires significantly less fastidious handling. At present, though, PCR is more expensive than viral culture. PCR is expected to replace viral culture in the near future as it becomes more readily available for routine clinical use.

Whenever the virus is detected, either by culture or PCR, the specimen always should be typed to determine if it is HSV-1 or HSV-2. This will facilitate safer-sex counseling and provide a prognosis for the clinical course. Genital reactivation of the virus is much less frequent with HSV-1, which rarely recurs with or without symptoms after the first year of infection. In contrast, genital HSV-2 continues to recur, often quite often, for many years. . . .

FAST FACT

The Centers for Disease Control and Prevention (CDC) estimates that 880,000 pregnant women in America are infected with herpes annually.

Pregnant Women Should Be Tested

Who should have HSV serologic testing? All women requesting sexually transmitted infection screening or requesting herpes testing, as well as any woman with a current or past sex partner with genital herpes. We also recommend HSV serologic testing in all patients with HIV infection due to interactions between these viruses that may facilitate HIV transmission. Along with some other experts, we advocate routine HSV serologic testing in pregnancy to prevent acquisition in the third trimester and subsequent neonatal herpes. The issues of cost and psychosocial impact are still being evaluated.

When interpreting test results, it's important to distinguish between HSV-1 and HSV-2 for prognosis and to distinguish between new versus established infection. This is particularly important in pregnant patients, because the risk of transmission to the baby is high only in new infections acquired in the third trimester. If a woman is seronegative for the type identified on culture or PCR, assume it's a new infection. . . .

Based on the unpredictable and largely asymptomatic nature of genital shedding of HSV, prevention of transmission can be challenging. However, we now have several proven methods to prevent transmission. Key factors

A test kit manufactured by OraQuick requires only a single drop of blood to do an STD test. (David McNew/Getty Images)

to prevent genital herpes transmission include disclosure to sexual partners, condom use, and antiviral suppressive therapy in the infected partner, each of which [cuts in] half the risk of HSV transmission. Therefore, we advise patients to disclose that they have genital herpes before initiating sexual activity and use condoms regardless of signs or symptoms of genital herpes, and that the source partner receive antiviral suppressive therapy.

Pregnant Women Should Not Be Tested for Herpes

Adam C. Urato and Aaron B. Caughey

Recent proposals in the medical community to implement universal testing of pregnant women for the herpes virus have provoked sharp opposition from some quarters. In the following article two professors of medicine, who specialize in pregnancy, argue that universal testing would be a bad policy. There is little evidence that testing all pregnant women would do much good, they argue, while the potential for harm is clear. A positive test for herpes would lead to unnecessary caesarian-section births and to drug treatments whose effects during pregnancy could be harmful. Ignoring previously acquired infections raises little risk of infecting the baby, because the mother passes antibodies to the fetus, they say. The medical community should also consider the social impact of informing millions of pregnant women that they are infected with herpes, the authors suggest. Adam C. Urato is an assistant professor in the Department of Obstetrics and Gynecology at the University of South Florida. Aaron B. Caughey is assistant professor in residence in the Department of Obstetrics, Gynecology, and Reproductive Sciences at the University of California at San Francisco School of Medicine.

SOURCE: Adam C. Urato and Aaron B. Caughey, "Universal Prenatal Herpes Screening Is a Bad Idea in Pregnancy," *Lancet,* vol. 368, September 9, 2006. Copyright 2006 The Lancet Ltd. Reproduced by permission of Elsevier.

Three articles in leading US obstetric journals have called for universal herpes simplex virus screening during pregnancy. We believe that on the basis of the evidence such a strategy would provide little benefit and could be harmful to pregnant women and their babies.

There are two main adverse outcomes related to herpes simplex virus infection in pregnancy: neonatal herpes simplex virus infection from exposure at delivery, and caesarean delivery for those women presenting in labour with a genital herpes outbreak. Proponents of universal prenatal herpes simplex virus screening argue that such screening will address these issues by identifying herpes simplex virus-2 positive women, who could then be offered antiviral prophylaxis to

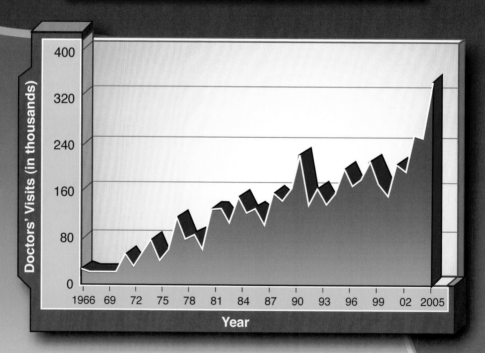

Doctors' Visits for the Treatment or Diagnosis of Herpes Are on the Rise

Doctors' Visits (in thousands)

Year

Taken from: Centers for Disease Control and Prevention, "STD Surveillance 2006, Figure 40. Genital Herpes–Initial Visits to Physicians' Offices: United States," November 13, 2007.

prevent outbreaks at delivery, and, in turn, caesarean deliveries. Women found to be herpes simplex virus seronegative [uninfected] could take precautions in the third trimester to avoid infection (eg, avoid sexual intercourse or have herpes simplex virus-infected partners take antiviral medication or use condoms).

The problem with the above strategies is that with little evidence of benefit there is substantial potential for harm. First, it seems that the protective benefit from a caesarean delivery for women with recurrent outbreaks in labour is small. Women with recurrence have already passed protective antibodies to their fetuses and rates of neonatal infection in this setting are low (0–3%). In the Netherlands, for example, a caesarean is not done for recurrent outbreaks and the incidence of neonatal herpes there is rare, despite the fact that herpes simplex virus rates approximate those in the USA. Data from California further support these findings.

FAST FACT

The federal Centers for Disease Control and Prevention (CDC) states that "insufficient evidence exists to recommend routine HSV-2 serologic screening among previously undiagnosed women during pregnancy."

Drugs May Imperil Pregnancy

However, even if the policy of caesarean delivery for a recurrent outbreak in labor is accepted, there is no compelling evidence for antiviral prophylaxis [prevention] for all herpes simplex virus-2 positive women. The main subgroup of women for whom antiviral prophylaxis with [antiviral drug] acyclovir has been shown to decrease caesarean rates are those women with a herpes outbreak during pregnancy. Providing antiviral prophylaxis to all herpes simplex virus-2 positive pregnant women would mean treating about one in four women. There is little long-term safety data about antiviral use in pregnancy and the small amount that does exist predominantly concerns acyclovir and not valacyclovir [another antiviral drug]. The potential complications or idiosyncratic reactions that might arise from the treatment of 25% of all pregnant women are unknown.

Many experts think that prenatal screening of pregnant women for herpes simplex provides little benefit and may even harm pregnant women. (Joel Robine/ AFP/Getty Images)

Little Risk of Transmission

Furthermore, women who test positive for herpes simplex virus-2 seem to be at lowest risk for having a newborn baby with herpes infection. Additionally, herpes simplex virus-2 positive women, with no history or only a distant history of genital herpes, seem to be at low risk for an outbreak in labour leading to a caesarean—although there is little reliable data specifically addressing this subject. Universal testing would take these women, who seem to be at low risk for either neonatal herpes or caesarean delivery, and label them as herpes simplex virus-2 positive. This would likely lead to stigmatisation, tension in relationships, and an increase in caesareans because patients and providers would be concerned about herpes simplex and any perineal symptom or finding—whether herpes-related or not— could then prompt an intervention.

PERSPECTIVES ON DISEASES AND DISORDERS

Although a strategy of identifying all pregnant women who are herpes simplex virus seronegative and having them take precautions to prevent infection might seem workable in theory, in practice this is likely not to be the case. There is no evidence that obstetrical providers will be effective in getting partners tested or in changing the sexual behaviour of patients, key components of any such strategy. Certainly, before universal screening recommendations are made, a large prospective trial of interventions to prevent transmission to these seronegative women should be studied.

A Poor Investment

Four of five cost-effectiveness analyses have concluded that universal prenatal herpes screening is not cost-effective and several expert panels do not recommend the strategy. The Centers for Disease Control and Prevention Sexually Transmitted Diseases Treatment Guidelines, 2006, do not recommend herpes simplex virus screening for pregnant women. In 2005, the United States Preventive Services Task Force concluded that there were no benefits associated with universal herpes simplex virus screening in pregnancy. The Royal College of Obstetricians and Gynecologists (2002) and the American College of Obstetricians and Gynecologists (1999) also do not support universal herpes simplex virus testing in pregnancy.

Until new evidence emerges, the message to pregnant women and their obstetric providers should be clear: universal herpes simplex virus screening in pregnancy is not recommended. Prenatal screening for herpes simplex virus provides little benefit to pregnant women and has a substantial potential for harm.

CHAPTER 3

Personal Experiences with Sexually Transmitted Diseases

A Teen Comes to Terms with Herpes

Holly Becker

Trust is an essential part of any loving relationship. When it comes to sexually transmitted diseases, however, people often fall short of telling the truth. In the following essay a girl who trusted her boyfriend tells the story of how he misled her and infected her with the virus that causes herpes. She believed his claims that he was "clean" (disease-free) and that he would use a condom. When they were engaged in sex she realized that he was not using a condom, and she later found out that he had infected her. Scared and in denial, she did not seek a diagnosis or get help. Eventually, however, when the pain became overwhelming, her mother came to her aid. She sought a diagnosis, got treatment, and confronted her boyfriend "Derek" (a pseudonym she uses to keep his real name private). Holly Becker was eighteen when she contributed this essay to the teen-run Web site Sex, Etc. She lives in Carrollton, Texas.

His name was Derek [a pseudonym], and I knew him from work. He was 22 and I was 17. Tall and skinny, he wasn't the cutest guy, but his character

SOURCE: Holly Becker, "Herpes: My Story," *SexEtc.org*, April 15, 2005. Copyright © 2008 Answer, Rutgers University. All rights reserved. Reproduced by permission.

Photo on facing page. Trust is a big part of a loving relationship, but when it comes to sexually transmitted diseases, people often fall short of being truthful. (**Bubbles Photolibrary/Alamy**)

made him attractive. He was funny, very charismatic, and he treated me well. He made me feel like I was someone to be noticed. To guys at work, he would say, "Wow, boys, look at that girl. Isn't she somethin'?" He gave me special attention to boost my self-esteem. He would say other things like, "You're so beautiful." Whenever other girls were around, he'd ignore them and only pay attention to me. Derek was my friend, and I trusted him.

About a month after we started hanging out, we had sex for the first time. I asked him that question: "Have you been tested?" He swore to me that he had. "I'm clean," he said. He didn't get specific about when he was last tested. I still asked him to wear a condom.

No Condom

A little while into the sex, I could tell he hadn't put on a condom. I knew then that I'd made a mistake, but I didn't stop him. I was embarrassed and afraid of being rejected. I thought about treatable infections, like chlamydia, and figured that if Derek had anything, then I'd already gotten it and the damage was done.

I started noticing some differences with my body—pains and smells that hadn't been there before. Derek and I still slept together without a condom. I kept thinking that the damage was already done. And I wasn't serious with him; we were very casual. So I didn't say anything. I figured there was no way I could get anything serious, like herpes, HIV, or syphilis. I was also nervous. I'd never been to a gynecologist, just to my doctor for checkups, and I was too afraid to tell my mother what I was doing.

Increasing Agony

The symptoms were unbearable and the pain got worse. I couldn't urinate without screaming out loud. My abdominal pain brought tears to my eyes. While working alone one day, I got very sick. I called my mother and asked her to come get me. I finally told her about my symptoms. We went to a gynecologist first thing the next morning.

Thank God for my supportive mother. She held my hand while I screamed in pain as the doctor took a Pap smear and culture. It felt like torture. Imagine this: your entire insides are swollen and inflamed, and someone puts just a slight amount of pressure on that swelling and inflammation. It feels like someone just rammed a sword into you. I have never felt anything so horrible.

After seeing the open lesions that were down there, the doctor said that there was a good chance it was genital herpes. He was certain that I had a raging case of Pelvic Inflammatory Disease (PID), which is sometimes caused by an STD.

"Genital herpes?" I thought. "He must be wrong; he's just trying to scare me. Am I the type of girl who gets herpes? Who is?"

FAST FACT

Of the 18.9 million new cases of STIs (sexually transmitted infections) each year, 9.1 million (48 percent) occur among fifteen- to twenty-four-year-olds.

About the Virus

Herpes is a sexually transmitted disease that's caused by the herpes simplex virus (HSV). HSV-type 1, or oral herpes, normally causes fever blisters on the mouth or face. HSV-type 2, or genital herpes, usually affects the vagina, penis, and/or anus. Herpes viruses are usually "inactive" and cause no symptoms. But sometimes, the viruses cause "outbreaks" of fluid-filled blisters and lesions.

Once a person is infected with herpes, he or she has it for life.

Genital herpes is not uncommon. If you look at the percentage of adolescents and adults who have it, you might even consider it normal. Across the United States, 45 million sexually active people ages 12 and older—that's one out of five of the total adolescent and adult population—are infected with HSV-2. And genital herpes is more common in sexually active females—approximately one out of four of us are infected with it.

In the United States more than 45 million people aged twelve and over are infected with HSV-2. Use of condoms has been proven effective in reducing the risk of contracting herpes. (David J. Green/ Alamy)

But even though herpes is so widespread, the general feeling in society is that there's something really wrong with you if you become infected. Like you had to sleep with at least five people, instead of just the one person who gave it to you. The common perception is that you're obviously a "slut" if you get genital herpes. But I slept with one person and I got it.

Most people don't know that you can live with and manage herpes. Every once in a while, especially when you're stressed, you'll get outbreaks of tiny lesions or blisters on your genitals. If you have sex during this time, you're likely to transmit the virus to your partner. You can also transmit herpes to a sexual partner before and after you break out in sores, until the sores have healed. But you can't get herpes from a toilet seat, a towel, or clothing. These are myths.

If you're going to have oral sex or intercourse, always use a latex condom or dental dam the correct way. But remember, condoms don't completely protect you from herpes. If a guy has genital herpes, for instance, the condom won't cover lesions that appear on his scrotum or testicles. So abstaining from sex is sometimes the best thing to do.

Confronting the Partner

I ended up confronting Derek. I felt he needed to know what he had done, so he would use a condom from then on. We dated for a little while longer. Then he decided to go back to his ex-girlfriend. We're no longer friends.

Each day, I try to deal with the fact that I have herpes. And when people put me down or treat me like I'm different, it makes coping with it even harder. Herpes has especially changed my life when it comes to relationships. You never know when you're supposed to tell someone and if they will freak out.

After I was diagnosed, I started dating an old boyfriend again. When I told him about it, he acted like he was fine with it. But the next day, he started being really distant. Then I found out he told a lot of people, which really hurt. Whenever someone acted weird toward me, I wondered if it was because they knew.

One time, my old boyfriend's friend was in class with me and started talking really loudly about me to another person in the room. "Yeah, she's a whore and has herpes from some guy she knew for like an hour," he said. "Guess that taught her to keep her legs shut." I had to leave the room I was crying so hard.

When I first got the virus, I thought, "Who would want to ever marry a girl with herpes?"

Openness Helps

But the more I am open with people about it, the more I learn that it's OK. I know that someone will love me for me and not care that I have herpes, because the virus doesn't make me who I am. Still, sometimes I avoid relationships altogether, for fear of rejection. And that makes me lonely.

So, think about my story when you're having sex. Ask your future partners the hard questions, too. Ask them about their sexual past, when they were tested, for what, and, since then, what they've done to protect themselves.

And think about my story when you hear that someone has an STD. Most likely, if they have one, they are scared and lonely, and could use a friend.

A Woman Dying of Cervical Cancer Tries to Help Others Avoid Her Fate

ABC World News Tonight

Cervical cancer is the second most common form of cancer for women. However, it can usually be detected and successfully treated through an annual Pap test. In the following article *ABC World News Tonight* profiles a woman whose tests were misdiagnosed. By the time the correct diagnosis was made, it was too late for Heather Burcham. Doctors told her she had only months to live. The thirty-one-year-old, otherwise fit young woman decided to dedicate the remainder of her life to raising awareness of the possibility of preventing the disease. In particular, she advocated for the newly approved vaccine against human papillomavirus (HPV), a sexually transmitted infectious agent responsible for most cervical cancers. Texas governor Rick Perry publicly commended her for her courage in speaking out in the face of a death sentence from her disease. A former teacher from Houston, Burcham died of cervical cancer on July 21, 2007, five months after *ABC News* featured her as the Person of the Week.

There's a heated debate going on in many states over whether a vaccine that can prevent cervical cancer should be given to all young girls. Since cervical

SOURCE: *ABC World News Tonight*, "Person of the Week: Heather Burcham," *ABC News*, February 23, 2007. Copyright © 2007 ABC News Internet Ventures. Reproduced by permission.

cancer can be sexually transmitted, some believe requiring the vaccination might lead to young girls becoming sexually active. Others believe the vaccine is too new and not enough is known about it. More than 30 states are now debating the merits of requiring vaccination.

Our person of the week has a very strong opinion on this issue. She is dying of cervical cancer.

Heather Burcham is 31 years old. She was misdiagnosed at 26, and by the time she knew she had cancer, it was too late for any treatment to be effective.

Heather Burcham, with only months to live, testifies at the Texas State Capital in Austin in favor of the state's HPV immunization program for Texas schoolchildren. (AP Images)

"I don't want to have lived in vain. I don't want my life to have no purpose whatsoever. And if I can help spread the word about cervical cancer, and the HPV [human papillomavirus] vaccine, then I haven't lived in vain. . . . I think that they didn't want to tell someone so young and in such good health that they had cancer . . . let alone, they were going to die," says Burcham.

Any Age or Race

Burcham understands there are real questions about the vaccine. People have worries and concerns, and she just wants to make sure people educate themselves about cervical cancer, a cancer that kills 3,700 American women every year. And she does that by telling her own story.

> **FAST FACT**
>
> If cervical cancer is detected early, the chances of survival are excellent. When detected early, the five-year survival rate for cancer of the cervix is 92 percent.

"It can happen to women as early as 18 or 21. Cancer knows no age, knows no race, it knows no gender. It can happen to anyone, and I just beg mothers out there to please research. Please find out all you can about the vaccination before you make up your mind," Burcham says, weeping.

These days Burcham's life is not entirely about a cause. It's about extracting every last bit of joy from every day she has. Her own parents are out of the picture, so when she lost her apartment and health insurance, she was taken in by friends. These friends are now her family.

"Heather's a pretty amazing little girl. I think everybody's amazed how tough she is," says one friend, Judge Norman Lee.

Lee's wife, Mary, adds, "We take one day at a time, and the good days are fewer and fewer between. There are more bad days than good days. As the disease progresses, unfortunately [it] will get worse, but we take the good days and we run with it."

Enjoying Her Last Days

Burcham has since started to enjoy sky diving and traveling, sometimes to New York. And the hope is, next week the Lee family will take Burcham on a cruise. Lisa, the Lees' daughter, says, "Everything we do with Heather, I realize, is going to be her first time—first and last."

Burcham realizes her condition gives her certain freedoms. She says, "For example, ice cream for breakfast. You know, of course, I'm going to let myself have what I want, whenever I want."

And what does she say to those of us who are healthy? What lessons can we learn?

"Maybe just that, how lucky you are, that you get to wake up every day, and it's not in chronic pain. It's not being exhausted, or . . . falling asleep while you're eating. That you get to enjoy each moment," says Burcham, "Some people say, 'How do you do it?' How do you wake up every morning? And I say, 'What choice do I have?' You don't have a choice. You have to wake up each morning, but you choose how you do it—if you're going to do it happy, or if you're going to do it upset. And I choose to live my days happy, and trying to make a difference."

An African American Drill Sergeant Tells of Life with HIV

Robert Mintz, interviewed by Laura Jones

Globally, HIV infects people of every description, but in the United States there are two populations that are disproportionately affected: gay men and African Americans. In the following interview we hear from a man who is both gay and black. Robert Mintz did not find it easy to speak up. He feared the reaction of his parents if he revealed that he was gay, and he knew that many in the African American community are not tolerant of homosexuality, much less HIV-positive men. Fortunately, he found that his father and others close to him were very accepting, and he found the strength to speak out. Now retired, he says he is motivated to continue telling his story by the desire to stop the needless deaths of young people, especially in the African American community. Mintz is a Vietnam veteran and former drill sergeant who now lives with his partner in Kansas City, Missouri. He gave this interview on the occasion of winning an HIV Leadership Award.

SOURCE: TheBody.com, "HIV-Positive Retired Drill Sergeant and Vietnam Vet Raises Awareness in the African-American Community," 2005. Reproduced by permission.

*L*aura Jones: *What made you decide to speak out publicly about your HIV status?*

Robert Mintz: Well, to be honest, I decided to speak out publicly about my HIV status because there are too many African Americans dying from this disease. I went public to say "AIDS is alive and well in the community, so stop sticking your head in the dirt."

What do you think is unique about your story?

I'm an African-American male who served in the military as a leader of men and women. I'm speaking out for veterans who have served their country and have been infected with HIV. When the military started testing for HIV, I was the testing coordinator for a unit of 500. There were several people in my company whose test results came back "questionable," including me.

What do you think is unique about the audiences you try to reach when you speak out?

Too many communities are led by fear and ignorance, and this is especially true in African-American communities. There's been a change in recent years, because most ministers blocked us out until around five years ago. Now they're starting to let us come in and talk with the congregation. This is good, because for too long ministers didn't know how to talk with their parishioners about HIV/AIDS and people were mistreated. This is changing. Ministers are getting training, not only to work with people who are infected, but also with people who are affected. HIV-positive people and their families are getting educated and being treated with compassion.

What's the best thing about sharing your story with others?

The best thing about sharing my story with others is just standing up and saying, "I am somebody, and I am not ashamed" and also, "There is life after this diagnosis, and there is hope." And to those who are HIV-negative, telling them, "You *don't* want to wear these shoes."

What's the worst thing?

The, worst thing is that people are not heeding the message, and they are dying needlessly. You just keep trying, and you hope you make a dent in the wall for those who will hear.

Acceptance by Loved Ones

What do your relatives feel about you speaking out?

My relatives are 100 percent behind me—they want to be educated.

I want to say something about my parents. Concerning my sexual orientation, when I came home from Vietnam and decided I had to come out to my father, I was scared of how he'd respond. I took him to a park, because then if he was going to do anything he'd have to do it in public, you know? Before I even opened my mouth, he said, "Son, God gave you to me, and nothing's gonna take you away from me." I told him, "Your son's gay," and he said, "Your point is?" So when they learned about my diagnosis, they did not say, "I don't know you." They said, "What do you want us to do, besides keep loving you?" They spoke out whenever they heard prejudice against HIV-positive people or gay people.

What does your partner/spouse feel about you speaking out? Has he spoken out in any way as well?

I've been with my spouse, Jim, for 12 years. Jim has a family, and his wife and I are best friends. His sons are my stepsons. He realized his orientation and left home before we met, but when we got serious, I met his family and they were very warm to me. His sons said, "Just don't give Dad that disease," and I promised I wouldn't—that was unique. But when I got sick, I was overwhelmed by their generosity. They've been a positive in my life.

What have you learned since you began speaking openly about your HIV status—about yourself? About HIV? About

> **FAST FACT**
>
> The U.S. Army periodically tests all soldiers for HIV. It does not automatically discharge those found to be HIV positive, but it does place restrictions on their assignment to other units and limits their options for training.

other people either with or without HIV? How has speaking out helped you, and how have you changed as a result?

Speaking out makes me more confident about my life. I would wear a neon sign if I thought it would help, because, really, what can you do to me? Early on, I grew strong through knowledge. I wanted to learn how to live with this disease. Now I try to pass that strength on to others.

Coping with Diagnosis

Can you describe your feelings when you were first diagnosed? Did you feel differently a few months down the road? How long do think it takes to really process the diagnosis?

Total fear and shock. As I said before, I was tested through the military testing system, while I was testing coordinator for my unit. People came through in groups, got their blood drawn, and went away. My test was one of the ones that came back questionable. The doctor said, "Your test is positive; you've got four months to live. Gather up your stuff; you're gonna die," while my commander and I just stood there with our mouths wide open. They sent us to Georgia for confirmatory testing, and lots of people had come up positive. There was no compassion from the Army medical staff.

Because of the time frame, people were dying right and left. I figured I was going to die, too, but after four months passed I said, "Well, I'm still here, so I've got to start paying attention."

Any tips for those who are newly diagnosed?

Seek understanding. Seek support from trusted friends and family, and start educating yourself about HIV.

Sex Without Condoms

If you want to, can you share how you believe you acquired HIV?

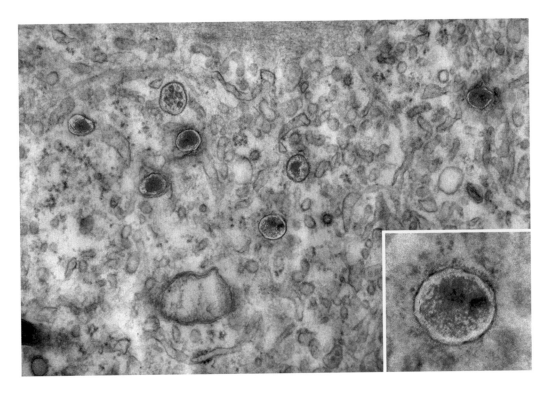

Promiscuous sex! We were having a good time back then! No one used condoms, because VD was the worst that could happen to you, and then you just got your bullet and 14 to 18 days later you could go back out and play.

What do you believe was your biggest risk factor?

Sex. I did the wild thing, you know, and I got caught. . . .

How do you maintain a positive outlook?

Let me say this: I am a faith-based person. God kept me here to do this work. Each time I got through a crisis, I figured, "God got me through that, so I must have something to do here. I better pay attention." I believe God's doing what he needs to do through me, and God doesn't make trash. It's true that we don't always act right, mostly because we're afraid and we want to be in power. But I want to empower! And if everyone gets to outlive me, great! . . .

This transmission electron micrograph shows human immunodeficiency virus (HIV) particles (orange) in a host cell. The virus attacks CD4+ T-lymphocytes (green), white blood cells that are a crucial part of the body's immune system. It enters the cell and hijacks the cell's machinery to copy itself. The cell dies when the virus clones burst from it, which weakens the immune system. (**Thomas Deerinck, NCMIR/Photo Researchers, Inc.**)

Treatment

What HIV treatments have you been on, if any?

Oh, I've been on just about every drug they have—AZT (Retrovir), ddI (Videx), d4T (Zerit), Fuzeon (T-20), Sustiva (efavirenz), Crixivan (indinavir), everything. I've had PCP pneumonia five times, and now I'm allergic to Bactrim so I have to do pentamidine every 30 days.

The worst side effects I've had are the puking and the diarrhea, and for a while I had to have transfusions every other week for anemia. I've had weight loss. I had side effects from Sustiva, but I kind of liked it! The trick with that is I took it with a sleep medication—I'd go to bed dizzy, but then I'd just fall asleep. For a lot of people, it works if you just don't take it until you're going to bed.

How often do you see your doctor? How did you choose your care providers?

Right now I see my doctor once a month for the pentamidine, and every three weeks or so to monitor my counts because of the resistance. There's some new drugs coming out soon, Truvada (tenofovir + FTC) and tipranavir so we're holding off new treatments for now.

You don't get to choose your providers in the Veterans Affairs (VA) system, but it's free. I had the choice of going with the VA and having everything covered 100 percent under my disability, or going to a civilian facility at cost.

What kind of relationship do you have with your care providers?

We're a team. Treatment through the VA has gotten better. I was only the 51st AIDS case to come through the VA, and some of the staff I see now have been there the whole time. I've had to school some people over the years. I was around for the shoving food under the door at the hospital and the staff wearing space suits and all that, so I've seen it. But I've had four doctors now through the VA that have been excellent, and my present infectious disease doctor is wonderful.

Do you have any health/wellness regimen that you feel helps you keep healthier?

I walk. I used to be a drill sergeant, fitness trainer, run 10 to 20 miles a day, climb mountains. That was then, but I'm still active. I still get good exercise. . . .

Receiving the HIV Leadership Award

What was your first reaction when you were told you'd received this award?

I was very surprised. Carol Ann, one of the infectious disease nurses, called me and told me she was nominating me and went on and on about things I do, especially encouraging vets and gay vets to speak out. Yes, I was surprised.

Who would you dedicate this award to, if you could?

My father—and my spouse, Jim, if I could add a second person. He won't be my nurse—he's a registered nurse—but he says, "I'm your spouse! I'm not going to be your nurse, too!" He's shown me nothing but compassion, love and understanding. He's been my rock.

GLOSSARY

abstinence To refrain from sexual intercourse.

AIDS Acquired immunodeficiency syndrome, which denotes a usually fatal destruction of the immune system caused by the human immunodeficiency virus (see HIV).

antibiotic A medication that is capable of killing bacteria but not viruses. Useful for treating bacterial infections, including some sexually transmitted diseases, provided that the bacteria have not evolved resistance to it.

asymptomatic Having an infectious organism within the body but showing no outward symptoms.

bacteria Tiny, single-celled organisms that are responsible for some sexually transmitted diseases.

cervix The narrow neck at the top the vagina that forms the entrance to the uterus.

chlamydia A bacterial infection that is among the most widespread of sexually transmitted diseases in the United States. It is particularly dangerous for women because it often leads to sterility.

condom A thin sheath of latex, polyurethane, or other material that is worn over the penis during sex as a contraceptive and as protection against transmitted diseases.

contraceptive A substance, device, or method capable of preventing conception or pregnancy.

diagnosis   The determination by a doctor or other qualified health-care provider of what is causing a set of symptoms.

genital herpes   A sexually transmitted disease caused by the herpes simplex virus. It causes genital discharge, blisters, and painful open sores. Symptoms periodically recur throughout an infected person's lifetime.

genital warts   Warts that appear on or near the penis or vagina. They are caused by the human papillomavirus (see HPV).

gonorrhea   A bacterial disease that may or may not present symptoms but if left untreated can lead to pelvic inflammatory disease in women.

HIV   Human immunodeficiency virus, the AIDS-causing virus that attacks the immune system cells, leaving a person helpless against other infections. HIV is most commonly transmitted through unprotected sex, though it can also be transmitted through blood passing from one person to another.

HPV   Human papillomavirus, a type of sexually transmitted virus that causes warts on the genitals. Some species of the virus cause cervical cancer in women.

latent   A type of infection that is hidden, such as latent syphilis.

pelvic inflammatory disease   A female condition usually caused by a sexually transmitted disease that spreads from the vagina into the pelvic cavity, where it can cause sterility or even death.

semen   The male ejaculate that contains sperm.

sperm   The male reproductive cell that carries a father's DNA.

STD   Sexually transmitted disease; the term encompasses more than twenty bacterial and viral infections that are spread primarily through sexual contact.

STI   Sexually transmitted infection, a term now preferred in medical circles to STD because it includes infections that are latent but hazardous to others.

syphilis   A bacterial STD that comes and goes, with each new stage being more destructive than the last. If left untreated, syphilis causes mental illness, blindness, and eventually death.

urethritis   An inflammation of the urethra, the tube that carries urine and, in men, semen out of the body. Many STDs cause urethritis.

uterus   The pear-shaped chamber within a woman's body where a fetus grows into a baby.

venereal disease   An antiquated term for an STD.

virus   A submicroscopic parasite that can only grow in living cells. Viral infections are generally incurable but can often be managed.

CHRONOLOGY

B.C.	**ca. 1780**	Hammurabi's Codes, the Laws of King Hammurabi, make the first known mention of a sexually transmitted disease (STD).
	ca. 400	Hippocrates, the founder of Greek medicine, writes an analysis of a sexually transmitted disease of the urethra.
A.D.	**ca. 170**	Greek physician Galen observes the effects of an STD that causes discharge and names it gonorrhea, meaning "flow of seed."
	1020	The Muslim scholar Avicenna publishes *The Canon of Medicine*, which includes references to STDs.
	1498	Explorer Vasco da Gama and his crew inadvertently bring syphilis to India when they arrive in Calcutta.
	1895	The prevalence of STDs in the British army peaks at 52 percent.
	1906	The American Society for Social and Moral Prophylaxis warns of the rapid spread of STDs among armed services personnel.
	1907	German scientist Paul Erhlich develops salvarsan, an arsenic-based drug, to treat syphilis.
	1918	In the midst of World War I, the U.S. Army discharges ten thousand men infected with incurable STDs; Congress establishes an office to fight "venereal disease" in the military.
	1935	A class of drugs called sulfonamides proves effective against gonorrhea.

1943   For the first time, penicillin is used to treat STDs, achieving cure rates of over 90 percent in the armed forces.

1983   HIV is identified as the cause of a newly recognized sexually transmitted disease called AIDS.

1985   First evidence emerges of HIV transmission from mother to infant.

1995   A "triple cocktail" of protease inhibitors and two other drugs proves effective in suppressing HIV in AIDS patients, thereby prolonging their lives.

2005   The CDC reports that three major STDs—chlamydia, gonorrhea, and syphilis—are on the rise again.

2006   A quarter century into the global AIDS epidemic, an estimated 25 million people have died and no cure is in sight.

2007   A new variant of gonorrhea proves highly resistant to antibiotics. Scientists warn that drug resistance may spread to other bacterial STDs.

ORGANIZATIONS TO CONTACT

Advocates for Youth
1025 Vermont Ave. NW,
Ste. 200
Washington, DC
20005
(202) 347-5700
fax: (202) 347-2263
www.advocatesfor
youth.org

Advocates for Youth supports programs that increase youths' opportunities and abilities to make healthy decisions about sexuality. It publishes the newsletters *Passages* and *Transitions* as well as fact sheets on STDs and AIDS.

**American Foundation
for AIDS Research
(AmFAR)**
120 Wall St.,
13th Flr.
New York, NY 10005
(212) 806-1600
fax: (212) 806-1601
www.amfar.org

AmFAR supports AIDS prevention and research and advocates AIDS-related public policy. It publishes several monographs, compendiums, journals, and periodic publications, including the *AIDS/HIV Treatment Directory*, published twice a year; the newsletter *HIV/AIDS Educator and Reporter*, published three times a year; and the quarterly *AmFAR* newsletter.

**American Sexually
Transmitted Disease
Association (ASTDA)**
PO Box 133118
Atlanta, GA 30333-
3118
(404) 616-5606
fax: (404) 616-6847
depts.washington.edu/
astda

ASTDA is an organization devoted to the control and study of sexually transmitted diseases. Its objectives include the control and ultimate eradication of STDs; support for research in all aspects of STDs, including medical, epidemiologic, laboratory, social, and behavioral studies; and to disseminate authoritative information concerning STDs. ASTDA publishes the journal *Sexually Transmitted Diseases* and offers numerous additional resources at its Web site.

**American Social
Health Association
(ASHA)**
PO Box 13827
Research Triangle
Park, NC 27709
(919) 361-8400
fax: (919) 361-8425
www.ashastd.org

ASHA, established in 1914, is a nonprofit organization that educates and advocates on behalf of patients concerning sexually transmitted diseases. ASHA serves the public, patients, providers, and policy makers by developing and delivering accurate, medically reliable information about STDs. ASHA sells numerous brochures, books, and other items addressing STDs through its online catalog.

**Centers for Disease
Control and
Prevention (CDC)**
1600 Clifton Rd.
Atlanta, GA 30341
(800) CDC-INFO
fax: (770) 488-4760
www.cdc.gov

A division of the federal Department of Health and Human Services, the CDC carries out research and promotes public understanding of health and quality of life issues. Its Division of STD Prevention provides national leadership through research, policy development, and support of effective services to prevent sexually transmitted diseases (including HIV infection) and their complications. The CHSTP, a program of the CDC, publishes fact sheets on STDs and the *HIV/AIDS Prevention Newsletter*.

Guttmacher Institute
1301 Connecticut Ave.
NW, Ste. 700
Washington, DC
20036
(202) 296-4012
fax: (202) 223-5756
www.guttmacher.org

The Guttmacher Institute is a nonprofit entity that seeks to advance sexual and reproductive health through an interrelated program of social science research, policy analysis, and public education designed to generate new ideas, encourage public debate, promote sound policy and program development, and inform individual decision making. Among the institute's publications are the books *Teenage Pregnancy in Industrialized Countries* and *Today's Adolescents, Tomorrow's Parents: A Portrait of the Americas* and the report *Sex and America's Teenagers*.

The Mayo Clinic
200 First St. SW
Rochester, MN 55905
(507) 284-2511
fax: (507) 284-0161
www.mayoclinic.com

The Minnesota-based Mayo Clinic has a reputation for excellence in medicine and for a commitment to health education for patients and the general public. Its Web site includes a section on the prevention of STDs through condom use and other relevant information.

National Institute of Allergy and Infectious Diseases (NIAID)
6610 Rockledge Dr.
MSC 6612
Bethesda, MD 20892-6612
(866) 284-4107
fax: 301-402-0120
www3.niaid.nih.gov

NIAID conducts and supports basic and applied research to better understand, treat, and ultimately prevent infectious, immunologic, and allergic diseases. NIAID research has led to new therapies and other technologies that address sexually transmitted diseases, among other pathologies. NIAID publishes a monthly newsletter, information on its research activities, and many informational publications, including *Sexually Transmitted Diseases: An Introduction* and *HIV and Adolescents*.

World Health Organization (WHO)
20 Avenue Appia
CH-1211 Geneva 27
Switzerland
www.who.int

WHO serves as the coordinating authority for health within the United Nations system. It is responsible for providing leadership on global health matters, including infectious diseases. It compiles international statistics on STDs, especially HIV/AIDS.

FOR FURTHER READING

Books

Amy Breguet, *Chlamydia.* New York: Rosen, 2006.

Charles Ebel, *Managing Herpes: How to Live and Love with a Chronic STD.* Research Triangle Park, NC: American Social Health Association, 1998.

Brett Grodeck and Daniel S. Berger, *The First Year: HIV: An Essential Guide for the Newly Diagnosed.* New York: Marlowe, 2007.

H. Hunter Handsfield, *Color Atlas and Synopsis of Sexually Transmitted Diseases.* New York: McGraw Hill, 2001.

Deborah Hayden, *Pox: Genius, Madness, and the Mysteries of Syphilis.* New York: Basic Books, 2003.

Lisa Marr, *Sexually Transmitted Disease: A Physician Tells You What You Need to Know.* Baltimore: Johns Hopkins University Press, 2007.

Christopher Michaud, *Gonorrhea.* New York: Rosen, 2006.

Christopher Scipio, *Making Peace with Herpes: A Holistic Guide to Overcoming the Stigma and Freeing Yourself from Outbreaks.* Sechelt, BC, Canada: Green Sun Press, 2006.

Eileen Stillwaggon, *AIDS and the Ecology of Poverty.* New York: Oxford University Press, 2006.

Samuel G. Woods, *Everything You Need to Know About STD, Sexually Transmitted Disease.* New York: Rosen, 1997.

Periodicals

Jan M. Agosti and Sue J. Goldie, "Introducing HPV Vaccine in Developing Countries—Key Challenges and Issues," *New England Journal of Medicine*, May 10, 2007.

Lawrence K. Altman, "Sex Infections Found in Quarter of Teenage Girls," *New York Times*, March 12, 2008.

David Brown, "HPV Vaccine Advised for Girls," *Washington Post*, June 30, 2006.

Stephanie Desmon, "STDs Hit Fourth of Teenage U.S. Girls; Study Finds That Most Common Ailment Is HPV," *Tribune Newspapers*, March 12, 2008.

Nigel Hawkes, "Syphilis Makes a Comeback but Doctors May Not Know It," *The Times*, March 18, 2008.

Miranda Hitti, "Study: Similar Sexually Transmitted Disease Rates Between Pledgers and Nonpledgers," *WebMD Medical News*, March 22, 2005.

Nicholas D. Kristof, "The Secret War on Condoms," *New York Times*, January 10, 2003.

Courtland Milloy, "Ignorance Is Bliss, and Then You Get an STD," *Washington Post*, April 2, 2008.

Randall Patterson, "Students of Virginity," *New York Times Magazine*, March 30, 2008.

Susan Reimer, "STDs Still a Threat to Many Teens," *Los Angeles Times*, March 18, 2008.

Carmen Sanchez, "Nattrass: AIDS Denial Still Prevails in South Africa," *Daily Princetonian*, April 8, 2008.

Science Daily, "Internet Remedies for Sexually Transmitted Infections Pose Significant Public Health Hazard," November 20, 2007.

Dawn Turner Trice, "Teens Have Sex but Don't Have the Facts," *Chicago Tribune*, March 17, 2008.

U.S. Food and Drug Administration, "First of a Kind in HIV Treatment," *FDA Consumer Magazine*, November/December 2006.

Claudia Wallis, "Saying Yes to the HPV Vaccine," *Time*, March 9, 2007.

INDEX